AF477618

NEW ART ON PAPER

NEW ART ON PAPER

Acquired with funds from the
Hunt Manufacturing Co.

Ellen S. Jacobowitz and Ann Percy
Biographies compiled by Janet Smith

Philadelphia Museum of Art   1988

CONTENTS

PREFACE

Any attempt to survey the visual arts of the past decade reveals a wildly diverse, even paradoxical, array of contrasts. Pure abstraction or expressive figuration, mass-produced images or highly idiosyncratic handmade objects, revolutionary materials or revisionist use of traditional methods, huge scale or minute detail —no single attitude, or even group of attitudes, to making art can be said to dominate, and they are all present in works on paper. Despite extraordinary changes in approaches to drawing and printmaking during the 1980s, those creative processes continue to reveal the personalities and inclinations of artists with particular immediacy and to encourage viewers to join with the artists in the exploration of new territory.

It was therefore an inspired, timely, and warmly welcome initiative on the part of the Hunt Manufacturing Co. to launch a series of grants in 1979, funding the acquisition of new art on paper by the Philadelphia Museum of Art. Nine years later, the Hunt Manufacturing Co. Collection at the Museum includes over forty objects by artists from England, Italy, Germany, Denmark, Canada, The Netherlands, and the United States, bearing witness to the true internationalism of the current scene. The works of art reflect the lively diversity of the field and represent many possible definitions of the terms "innovation" and "invention." Should one say that Richard Long's wonderfully eloquent abstract circles, made by the artist's bare feet in mud from the River Avon, with vivid reference to ancient ritual markings made by man in nature, are more or less innovative than the laconic sequence of lithographs by Barbara Kruger, which manipulate the bold photographic images and simplified messages of modern advertising? The point is to locate the sense of adventure that lies at the heart of each work.

The pleasure of this particular adventure into new art has fallen to the Department of Prints, Drawings, and Photographs. The fruitful collaboration between the Hunt Manufacturing Co. and the Museum began under the curatorship of Kneeland McNulty, and has brought intense exposure to contemporary work and equally intense discussions to the department over the past nine years. The curatorial staff, notably Ann Percy and Ellen Jacobowitz, working with drawings and prints respectively, have taken on the search for acquisitions with great enthusiasm, and the process has undoubtedly enriched their own involvement with contemporary work and artists even as their findings have enlivened the Museum's collections. The entire staff of the Print Department, as well as many other departments in the Museum, have contributed to this project. Denise Thomas and Faith Zieske, conservators of works on paper, have given much thought to the care and presentation of these welcome acquisitions. Phillip Unetic has provided the handsome design for this catalogue, which catches the lively spirit of its contents.

The Museum is deeply grateful to the Hunt Manufacturing Co., and in particular to George E. Bartol III, Former Chairman, Ronald J. Naples, Chairman and Chief Executive Officer, and William Parshall, Director of Community Affairs and Secretary to the Hunt Manufacturing Co. Foundation, not only for the farsighted and generous sequence of grants that funded first the acquisitions and then this exhibition and catalogue, but also for their own commitment to a spirit of adventure in the arts and to the cultural life of the city of Philadelphia.

Last, but foremost, we all salute the contemporary artists whose work gives audiences around the world a sense of true adventure, and we hope that the pleasures and excitement offered by the works of art in the Hunt Manufacturing Co. Collection will be contagious.

Anne d'Harnoncourt
The George D. Widener Director

Innis Howe Shoemaker
Senior Curator of Prints,
Drawings, and Photographs

FOREWORD

Innovation. Risk. These are concepts with which any organization must come to terms if it is to prosper in today's world.

In business, existing markets change and new markets develop. Recognizing the need to change and having the courage to act are the keys to continued success for a company focused on growth, particularly a smaller one. Growth through change demands the ability to innovate in order to respond as current markets change and new markets beckon. This innovation must reach into all elements of a company—products, strategy, organization. In some sense, the successful growing company is constantly remaking itself through innovation.

But innovation does not just happen. It requires vision and a willingness to take risks. Risk is not comfortable. It raises the specter of failure, but one cannot go beyond the familiar without tempting, and occasionally tolerating, failure. In the end, it is a question of attitude and expectations. At Hunt Manufacturing Co., innovation and prudent risk-taking have been critical in achieving our growth goals. We have always felt, as James Russell Lowell expressed it, that "not failure, but low aim, is crime."

Hunt has long had an interest in the arts, which has been expressed through its financial support of cultural groups. We have always felt that a commitment to the quality of life is significantly related to the quality of our business enterprise. The connection between business and the arts is sometimes a matter of debate, however—it is uncertain for some and distant for others. When business does get involved with the arts, it is with the familiar. But at Hunt we believe that one place where business and art do converge is in their insistence upon the importance of innovation and the necessity of taking risks to advance.

In many ways, the concepts of risk and innovation are central to the world of art. The artist, who reveals a bit of himself with each work, takes a risk every time he gives us this glimpse of himself. Ideas and their expression are the currency of the art marketplace. Artists create and innovate, and ultimately risk, as they explore new ideas, give new expression to old concepts, and provide a fresh perspective on and insight into ourselves and our world. The work may be serious or whimsical; the artist may be well established or new.

For the artists, the premium is on innovating to make a place for themselves. However, as in business, the risk of innovation is public acceptance, or the lack thereof. Art may be self-expression for the artist, but it derives its importance from its ability to influence our lives, and this can only happen through public attention. But the road from originality and innovation to public awareness and acceptance is fraught with detours and dead ends. It is a journey we at Hunt understand well because it is a route we have traveled often.

Thus, when in 1979 the subject of how Hunt might help the Philadelphia Museum of Art came up, we thought of the roles innovation and risk-taking play in our business life and concluded that funding the Museum's freedom to collect "adventurous and risk-taking" works on paper by contemporary artists would be a perfect opportunity to help a major institution innovate for the future. And, as important, it would also support artistic innovation. The project was started with the interest of my predecessor at Hunt, George E. Bartol III, and has been nurtured over the past nine years.

It is an important function for museums to interpret our world for us. Too often museums take the easier course of exhibiting and interpreting only what is past. Hindsight and distance make us all successful critics. Our intent was to give the Philadelphia Museum of Art the opportunity to reach beyond the security of the past. It has responded with relish to the challenge of looking ahead with this collection.

To acquire and interpret current works of art are indeed ambitious undertakings. One is inevitably left open to second-guessing. Artists who may have seemed like rising stars in 1980 may not have the same luster in 1988; others may already seem like old masters. Some works may leave the viewer perplexed regardless of when they were created and collected.

The formation of this collection gives the Museum the opportunity to help us understand today's art. While we may come to judge these works differently twenty years from now, what we learn today will help us appreciate the collection better in the future. This effort may even represent a small step toward promoting public understanding of contemporary art. If it accomplishes that goal, this undertaking will indeed be a "success."

Like all innovations, this project has engendered its share of qualms and doubts. The curatorial staff, the director, and the president of the Philadelphia Museum of Art have cheerfully and unfailingly addressed our concerns throughout this nine-year journey. They are to be commended. Although the collection has altered course in some ways since 1979, the integrity of the original intent of creating something "adventurous and risk-taking" has been scrupulously maintained.

Hunt Manufacturing Co. is proud to have been associated with this project. We hope this adventure will prove well worth the risk.

Ronald J. Naples
Chairman and
Chief Executive Officer
Hunt Manufacturing Co.

PLATES

In the early 1960s the University of California at Davis, where Robert Arneson now teaches, became a special locus for the phenomenon known as funk art, an eccentric, witty, antiformal, and often scatological mode of working shared by a number of Bay Area sculptors and painters. During this period Arneson developed an exuberant, irreverent, nonfunctional, Pop ceramic style that is a synthesis of painting and sculpture, influenced by the ceramic sculptor Peter Voulkos at Berkeley, who is widely recognized as having revolutionized American ceramic art by carrying an Abstract Expressionist aesthetic and vocabulary over into his work with clay. Arneson has been called the second most influential figure in California ceramics after Voulkos.

Arneson is less well known as a draftsman, mainly because his drawings before the late 1970s were preparatory in nature rather than ambitious in scale and finish. He reveals a remarkable facility for drawing, splashing and layering color and line and often intertwining words and phrases with his images. Like his sculptures—to which they are usually related in subject—Arneson's drawings reflect an ideological crisis through which he tries to synthesize humor and fine art. Visual and verbal puns combine in his work, often to powerful effect. Here the use of red, white, and black crayon, oil pastel, and acrylic and the lively arrangement of the rodents on the paper recall the techniques of old masters, such as the eighteenth-century French painter Antoine Watteau, whose work includes drawings in three colors (*à trois crayons*), with studies of heads, hands, or, as here, whole figures scattered gracefully across the page.

Rats
1981
Conté crayon, conté crayon wash, oil pastel, and acrylic on wove paper
33 x 44¾″ (83.5 x 113.5 cm)
1982-111-1

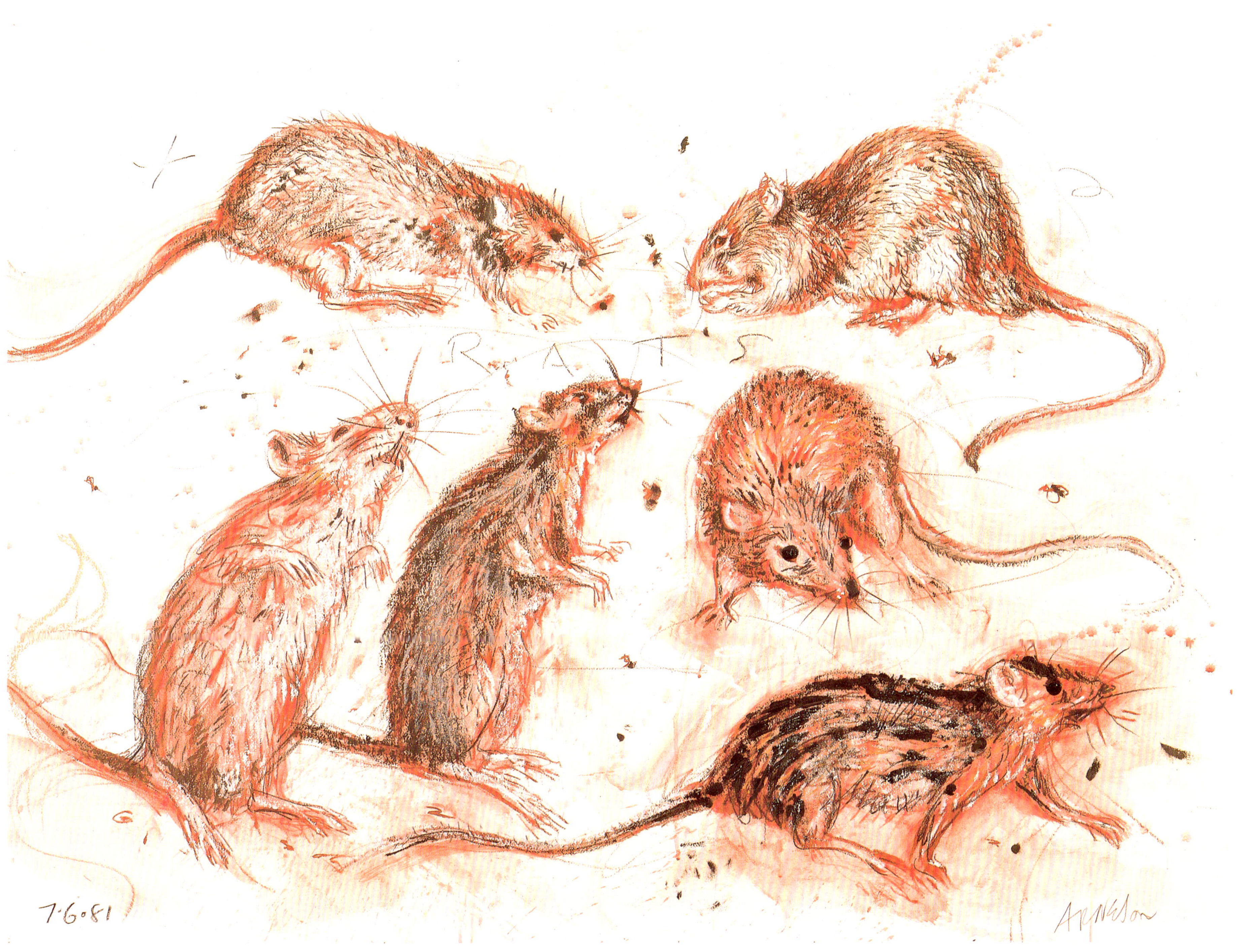

RATS
7·6·81

Alice Aycock is one of a number of contemporary artists, such as Mary Miss, Nancy Holt, Dennis Oppenheim, Jody Pinto, and George Trakas, whose works are architectural in scale and conception and usually are created for outdoor sites. During the 1970s Aycock's art evolved from Minimal or Conceptual "architectural sculptures"—incorporating elements such as stairs, tunnels, roofs, or walls constructed of earth, wood, or stone—to technology-based, fantasy "machineworks" made of industrial materials such as steel, rubber, glass, or aluminum, often motorized and charged with literary, historical, mythological, or personal references. Her drawings of that decade show a similar development from straightforward diagrams for projects to complex fantasy images.

Although they are literal isometric projections for three-dimensional sculptures, the artist views her drawings in a broader conceptual or philosophical sense, as means of defining different ways of seeing the world, as well as of effecting the particular combination of verbal and visual imagery that she seeks. Aycock culls ideas from wide reading in history, art history, philosophy, and literature. She uses poetic and evocative titles for her works—*The Great God Pan, How to Catch and Manufacture Ghosts, The Savage Sparkler*—and often writes short fantasy texts to accompany them. This spare, clean, precise rendering, executed in 1980 for a project for the plaza of New York's Seagram building, which was never realized, telescopes associations of the ancient Arcadian goat god with those of modern microelectronic circuitry, thus embodying Aycock's special conflation of science and magic.

The Great God Pan
1980
Graphite on Mylar
42 x 51¾" (106.5 x 132 cm)
1981-36-1

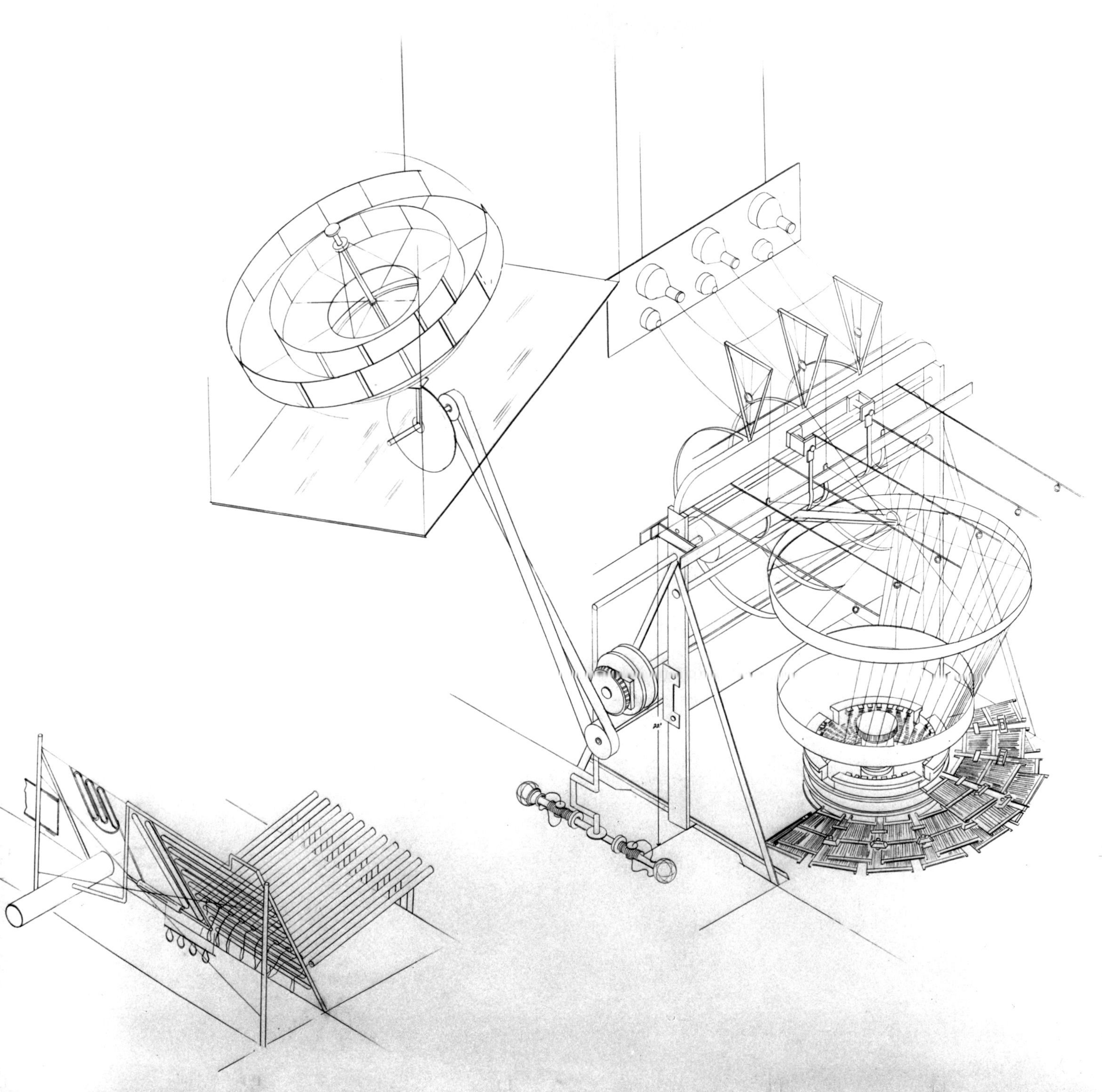

THE GREAT GOD PAN.
FROM THE SERIES ENTITLED
"THE MACHINE THAT MAKES
THE WORLD" SUBTITLED "PIE
IN THE SKY.

A PRELIMINARY PROPOSAL FOR THE
SEAGRAM'S PLAZA, NEW YORK CITY
- A MACHINE WITH MOVING PARTS.
FLUORESCENT TUBES & HOT COILS, IMMERSED
IN WATER & A HANGING PAN SUSPENDED
FROM A SHEET OF GLASS.

SCALE: 1' = 1/2'

John Baldessari is known for his use of imagery from the mass media. In this work, a still from a 1948 English gangster movie, *Black Dice*, serves as the inspiration for his nine etchings. Baldessari takes the photograph and divides it into nine sections, and then transforms these realistic sections into nine separate abstract compositions. The elegant etchings restate the concerns of the movie still: By isolating in each section an ordinary object such as a lampshade or a tuxedo, Baldessari directs the viewer's attention away from the interrelationships of the actors. The abstract execution of the etchings reduces interest in the plot and focuses on the graphic process itself, and Baldessari pursues further the play of verbal and visual images. The sense of mystery conveyed in part by dialogue in the movie is suggested in *Black Dice* by a language of shadowy grays and blacks.

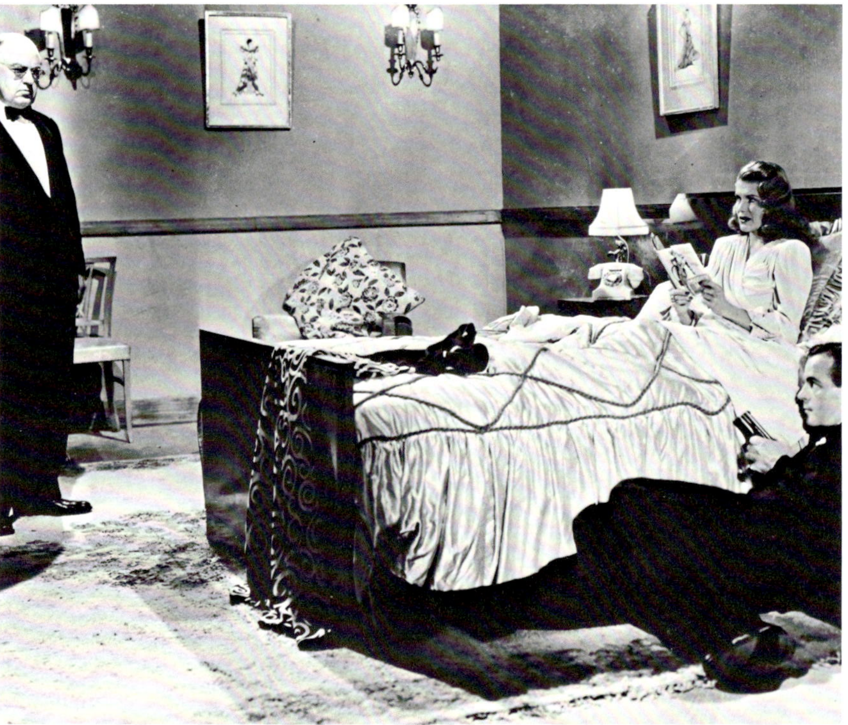

Black Dice
1982
Nine color etchings in drypoint, aquatint, sugar lift, soft ground, and photo-etching on Velin d'Arches paper, and photograph; edition 35 and 10 proofs; printed by Peter Kneubühler, Zürich; published by Peter Blum Edition, New York
6½ x 8″ (16.3 x 20.5 cm) plates
1983-27-1a–i

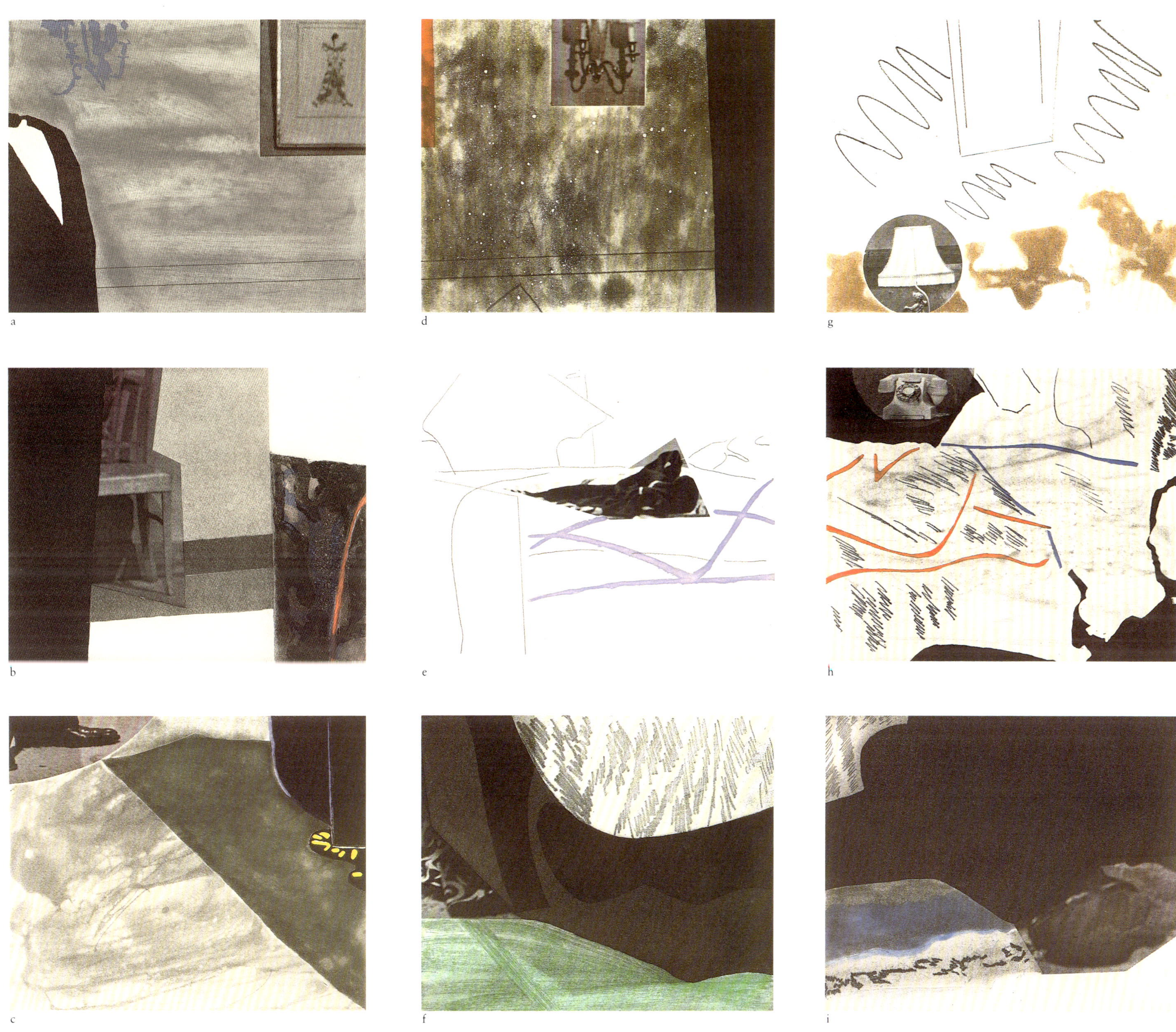

a

d

g

b

e

h

c

f

i

Based on a painstaking process utilizing eighty-six woodblocks and ninety-five silkscreens, Jennifer Bartlett's *At Sea, Japan* makes an important contribution to the current international woodcut revival and to the history of silkscreen. The artist herself drew the images on the screens, and cut the woodblocks following traditional methods learned from a Japanese printer.

In this ambitious multipartite panorama, which relates to a ninety-foot-long oil painting of the same name, the images seem to emerge in two stages, revealing various aspects of Bartlett's work: The sensuous and decorative arrangements of light-filled colors represent a new painterly freedom compared to her Minimalist and abstract works, and the lush depiction of the sea as it responds to changes in time and season shows her interest in the natural world of color, light, and reflection, as seen in Monet's paintings of waterlilies and haystacks. Against the lulling current, elliptical forms, perhaps swimmers, complement the colorful moods of nature, and in the third panel, where the draftsmanship is particularly energetic, suggest splashing in summer waters.

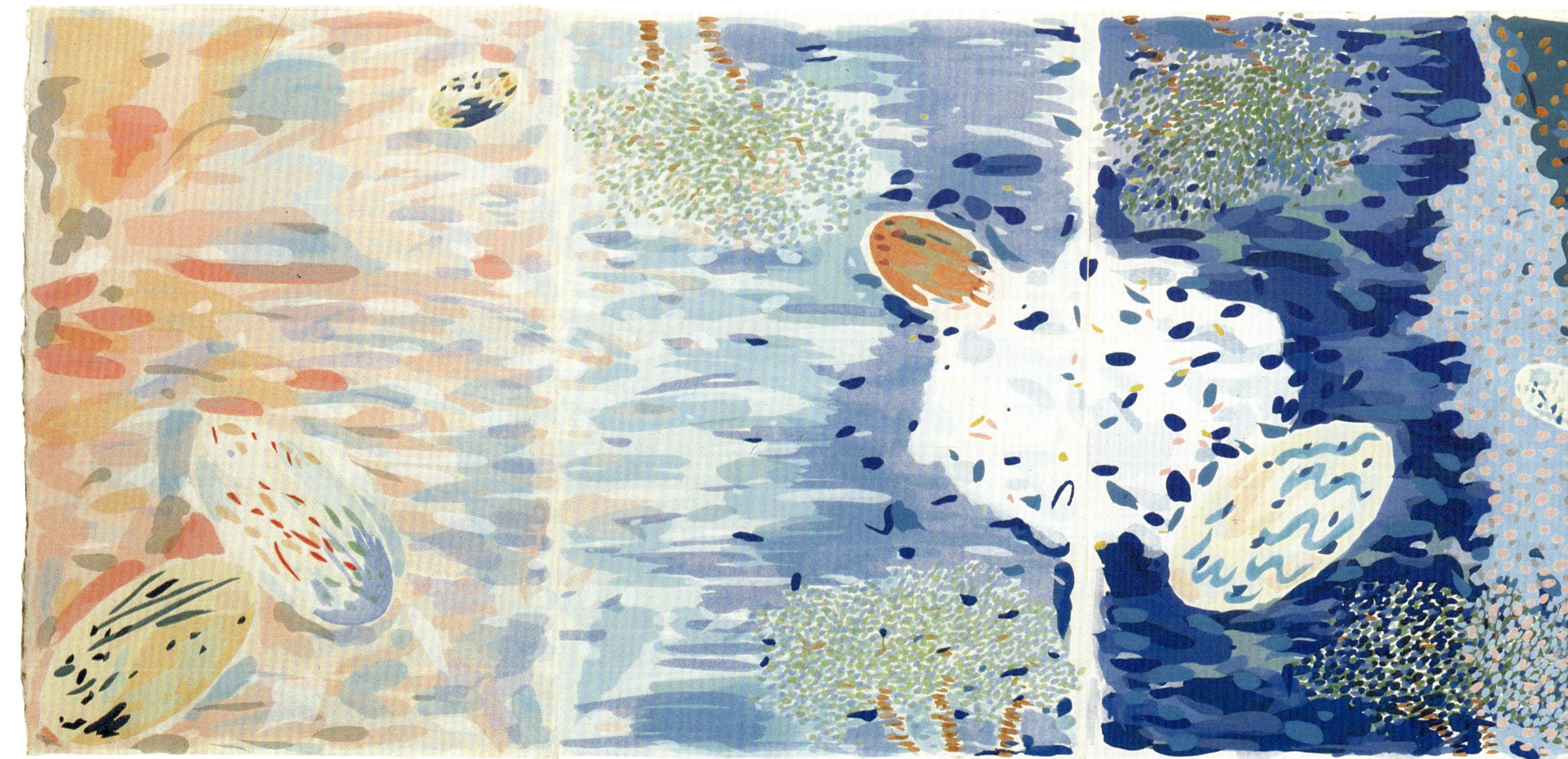

JENNIFER **BARTLETT**

At Sea, Japan
1980
Six-part color woodcut with screenprint
on Japanese handmade Kurotani Hosho
paper; edition 58; Simca Print Artists,
Tokyo
22½ x 99⅛" (57.6 x 251.8 cm) assembled
1981-14-1a–f

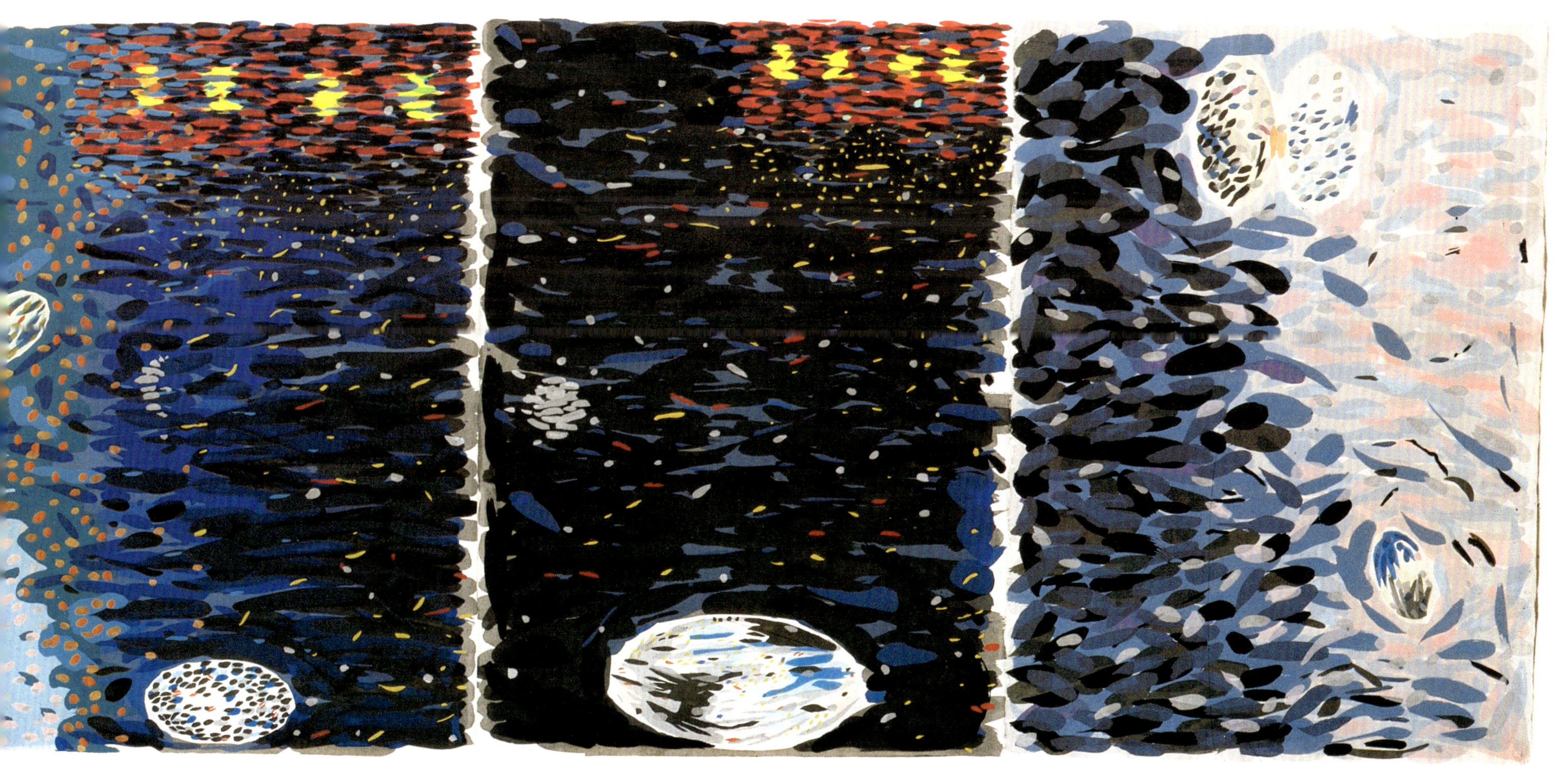

Since the early 1980s Lorenzo Bonechi's paintings and drawings have often been shown with those of a number of other Italian painters loosely grouped together as "anachronists," "painters of memory," or "cultivated painters," because their manners refer so strongly to the past, particularly to Italian Renaissance, Mannerist, Baroque, and Neoclassical painting, with strong overtones of surreal and dream imagery, eroticism and mystery. Most of the anachronists' pictures, however, have an overwrought, erotically charged, hothouse quality that is different from the cool ambiguity of Bonechi's works, which are rooted in a pure inspiration from his Tuscan origins. Bonechi's studio is in San Giovanni Valdarno, near Florence, only steps from Masaccio's birthplace. The little schematic hills of his landscapes are those of Duccio and Giotto, and the pale, geometrical loggias and arcades of his townscapes descend directly from the paintings of Fra Angelico.

Bonechi has developed a style notable for the dreamlike, introspective quality of his attenuated figures seen in isolation or in groups against landscape or cityscape backgrounds, executed with a distinctive draftsmanship built up from curling, wispily intertwined strokes of paint or chalk. He has been called a "contemporary theological painter," and his subjects are usually biblical, such as the Crucifixion, the Prodigal Son, Jonah and the Whale, or Jacob Wrestling with the Angel. Saint Galganus was a twelfth-century Tuscan hermit saint. This drawing for a painting now in a New York private collection evokes one of the dream legends associated with the saint's life, in which, as he slept on the bank of a stream, a lizardlike creature was seen to exit from his mouth, cross the stream on a sword placed there for that purpose, and return to enter his body again.

Saint Galganus
1985
Chalks on wove paper
47 x 59½" (120 x 150.4 cm)
1986-49-1

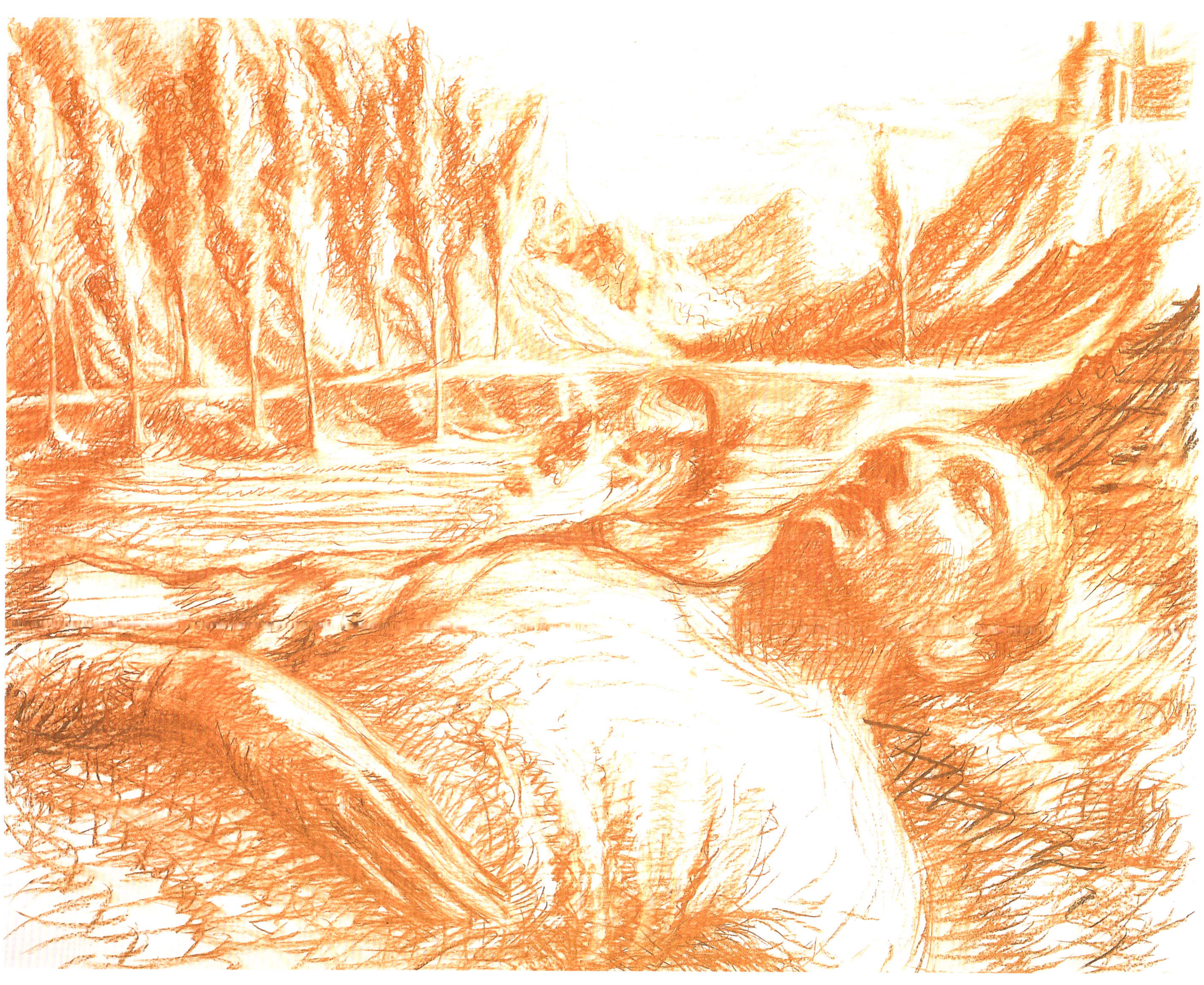

The subject of many of Francesco Clemente's works is his own face, hands, or body—as if he wished to maintain some individual strain of unity and cohesion within a large and varied oeuvre nurtured by a wide range of cultural stimuli. Never self-portraits in the literal sense, these works show the repeated motif of an individual figure transmuted into dream plays of various images through the use of vibrant colors, richly worked surfaces, subtle distortions of contours, drastic shifts in scale, and strange amputations and graftings one on another of figural, vegetal, animal, and landscape elements. The rich figuration of Clemente's images is fed by numerous and diverse sources in which boundaries of time and place are obliterated: In his personal culture, which is as literary as it is visual, the ancient mythographers of the classical past and the beat poets of contemporary America meet, as do old and new artistic traditions of India and the West.

Born in Naples, Clemente is part of that city's layering of cultures and of its sense of an unbroken connection to its Greek and Roman past. But he also spends part of the year in India, which he first visited when he was twenty-one, and in New York, where he took a studio when he was thirty. Within this rich mixture of world cultures, Clemente's art is specifically grounded in place: He uses techniques, materials, and imagery that respond to the character of the country in which he is working. His images are fresh, fierce, erotic, ascetic, and ambiguous; encountering them is like diving into a new ocean in a new land.

Italy
1983
Pastel on Rives wove paper
25¾ x 19" (66 x 48.3 cm)
1984-8-1

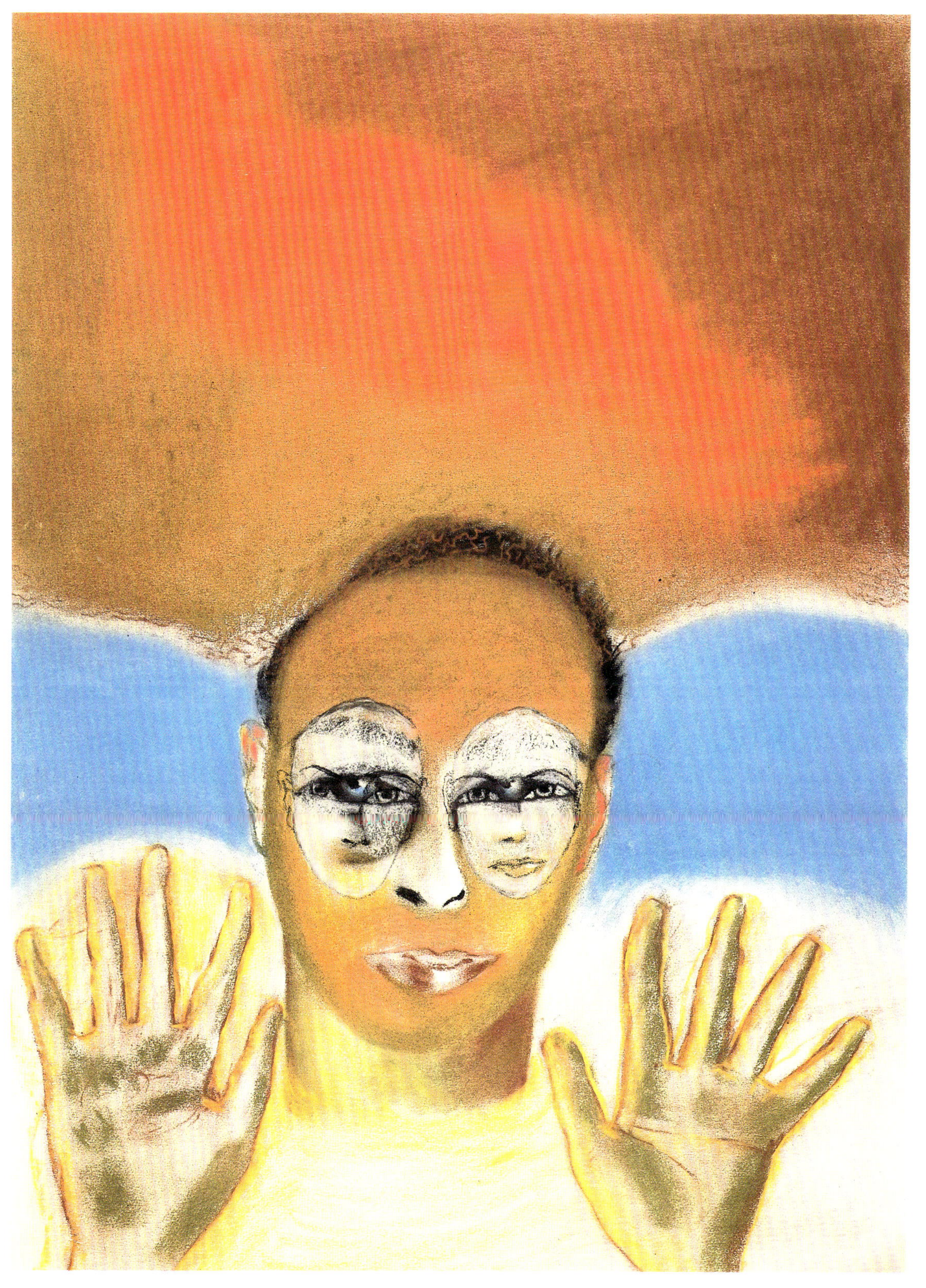

Enzo Cucchi is linked to Italian artists dating back to medieval times, and his imagery is inextricably bound to the Italian landscape. He has acknowledged an interest in Masaccio and Caravaggio, and more recent painters such as the Futurist Carlo Carrà and Surrealist Giorgio de Chirico. He has also been associated with two Italian art movements, Arte Povera in the 1960s and the Transavanguardia in the 1970s.

For Cucchi legends are "the only real things that exist, that will keep on existing."* In *A Dark Image* he refers to his homeland, Ancona, on Italy's east coast, as a place where the legends live, where the countryside represents the continuity of past and present, and where supernatural characteristics are attributed to the land. In order to grasp the elemental nature of such immaterial things, Cucchi limits the narrative by simplifying forms: The mountains convey a sense of spirituality and mystery; the black cloud is threatening in its unpredictable position; the monumental head, carried on a stretcher as in a funeral procession, suggests solemnity; and the trembling figure in the lower right corner expresses awe and vulnerability.

* Giancarlo Politi and Helena Kontova, "Interview with Enzo Cucchi," *Flash Art*, no. 114 (November 1983), p. 18.

A Dark Image
1982
Colored etching and aquatint on Fabriano Rosaspina paper; Arabic edition 30, Roman edition 6; printed by Valter Rossi at Vigna Antoniniana Stamperia d'Arte, Rome; published by Peter Blum Edition, New York
34½ x 54¼" (87.4 x 137 cm) plate
1983-29-1

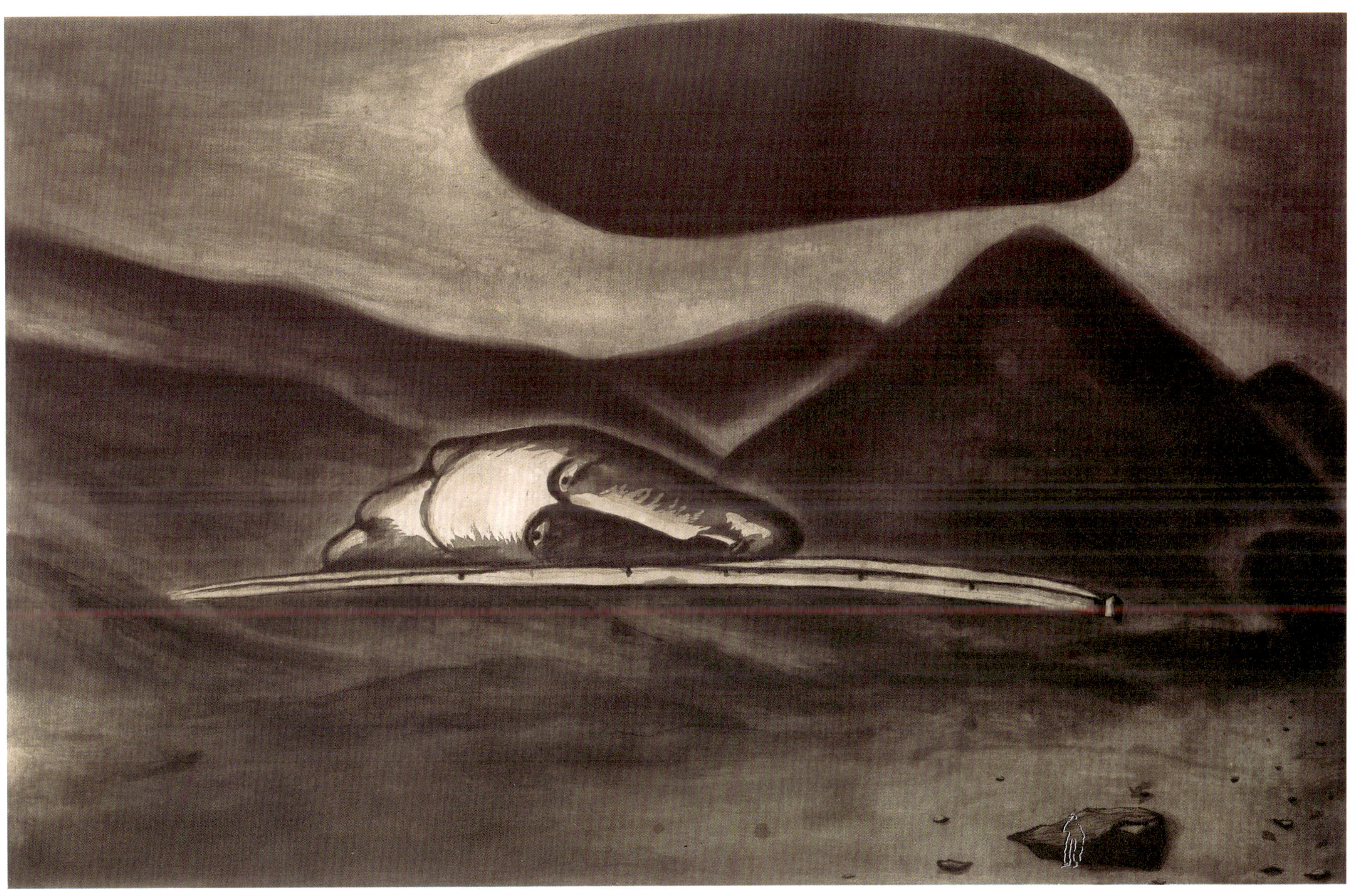

The issues that interest Jan Dibbets are those of a painter and of a photographer. He builds his photographic collages with a concern for perspective, illusion, time, light, and color, and questions the assumption that a photograph records reality exactly as it exists. Such concerns with perspective and perceived reality fit neatly into the tradition of Dutch art. The complex seventeenth-century interiors of Pieter Saenredam are a source for Dibbets's geometric and layered exposures, and Piet Mondrian's essential compositions in the twentieth century precede Dibbets's abstract ensembles.

Since 1967 Dibbets has used the photograph to manipulate perspective and rearrange actuality as seen in this edition of three untitled works. In a characteristic manner, he uses snapshots of a contemporary interior, that of the Kröller-Müller Museum in Otterlo, to construct composite circular images, and lithographic lines to extend the principal forms of the architecture into flat geometric configurations. Thus reducing realistic images to abstract compositions, he introduces perceptual and thematic ambiguities: What is real here, is it a clerestory or a series of trapezoidal forms? In these works Dibbets tackles the classical problem of reconciling the flatness of the picture plane with the depth of the image using photography as his medium.

JAN **DIBBETS**

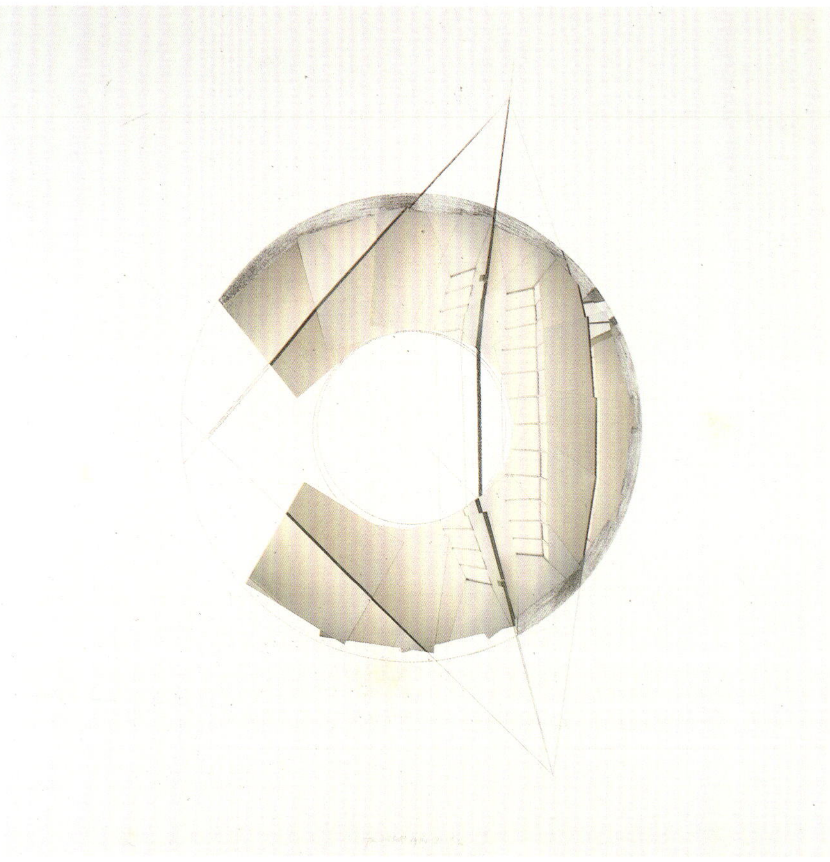

Untitled I, II, and III
1980
Three color lithographs with photocollage on board; edition 30; printed by Rento Brattingo, Amsterdam
28¾ x 28¾" (73 x 73 cm) sheets
1982-37-1a–c

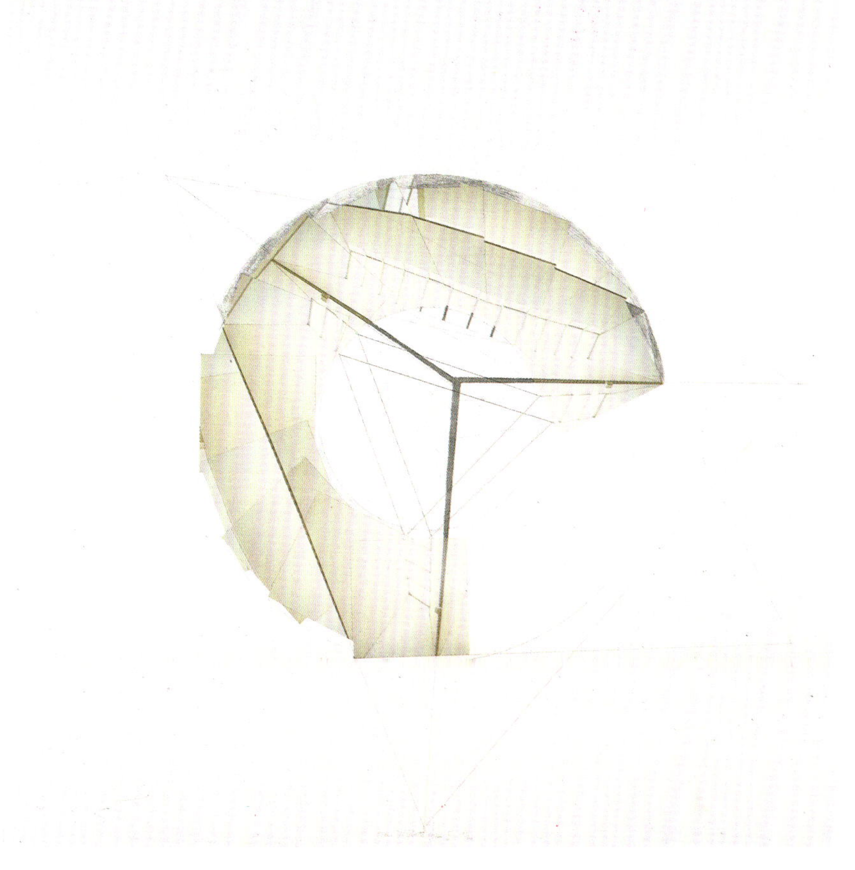

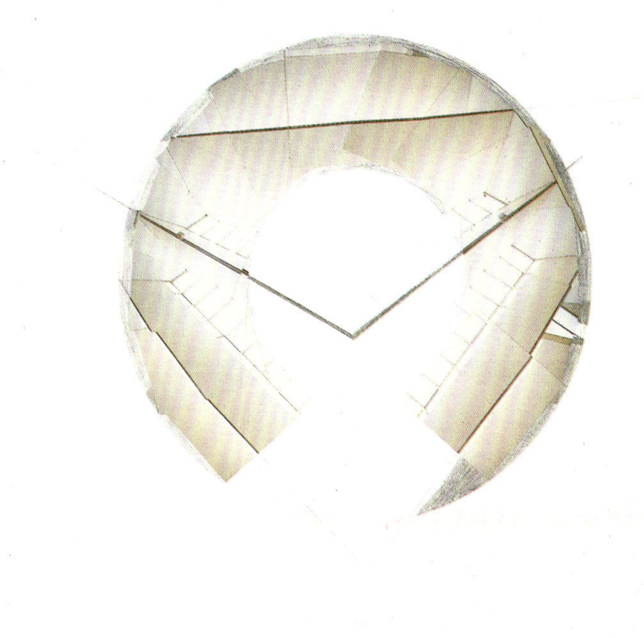

Like the work of such contemporary artists as Susan Rothenberg and Jonathan Borofsky, Eric Fischl's paintings and prints denote a resurgence of interest in figurative art. Fischl is known primarily for his disturbing and ambiguous narratives that explore and debunk suburban American life. In the *Year of the Drowned Dog*, the need to piece together fragments of a tragic story is graphically demonstrated in the use of six separate sheets, which might be shown as six independent prints or assembled together as seen here. The viewer stands before the arrangement as an anxious and alienated intruder, hoping to find meaning and cohesiveness by relating its separate parts. Fischl increases this disquieting effect by using different paper sizes, shifting the perspective, and interrupting the sky and coastlines. In an ironic comment on his sunny panorama, Fischl states: "Dreadful things often occur in beautiful light, which makes the event more tolerable."*

* Museum of Fine Arts, Boston, *The Modern Art of the Print* (August 1–October 14, 1984), p. 113.

ERIC **FISCHL**

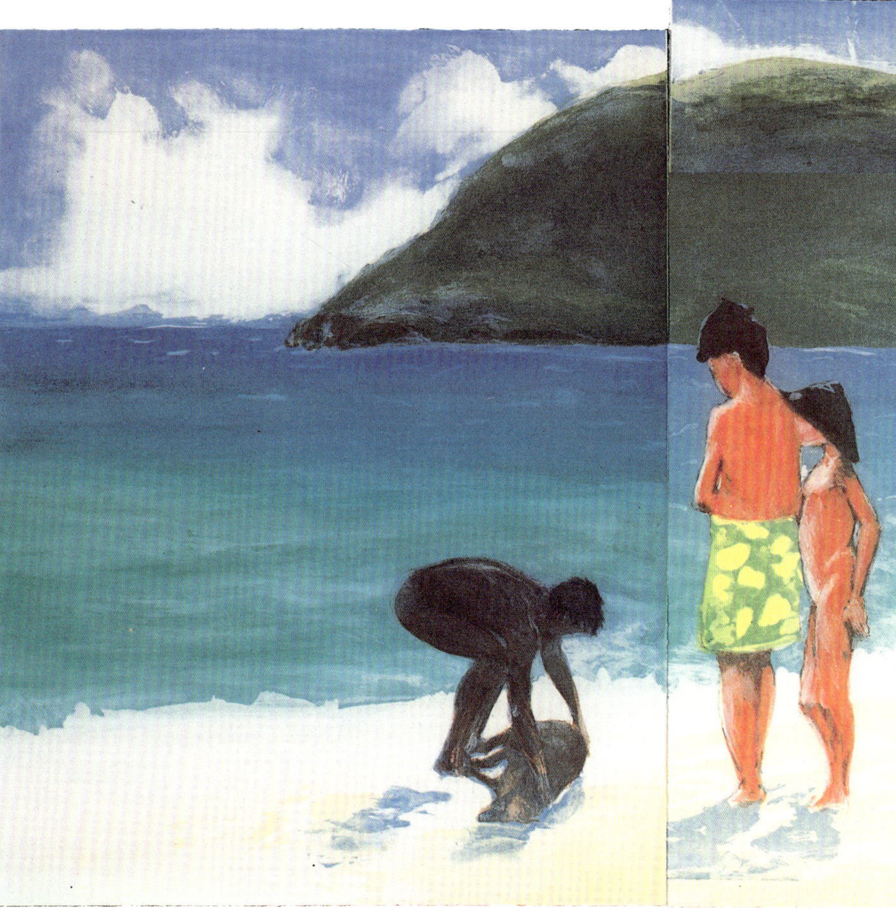

Year of the Drowned Dog
1983
Portfolio of six color etchings in aquatint, soft ground, drypoint, and scraping on Zerkall paper; edition 35 and 10 artist's proofs; printed by Peter Kneubühler, Zürich; published by Peter Blum Edition, New York
24⅝ x 70½" (62.5 x 179 cm) assembled
1983-164-1a–f

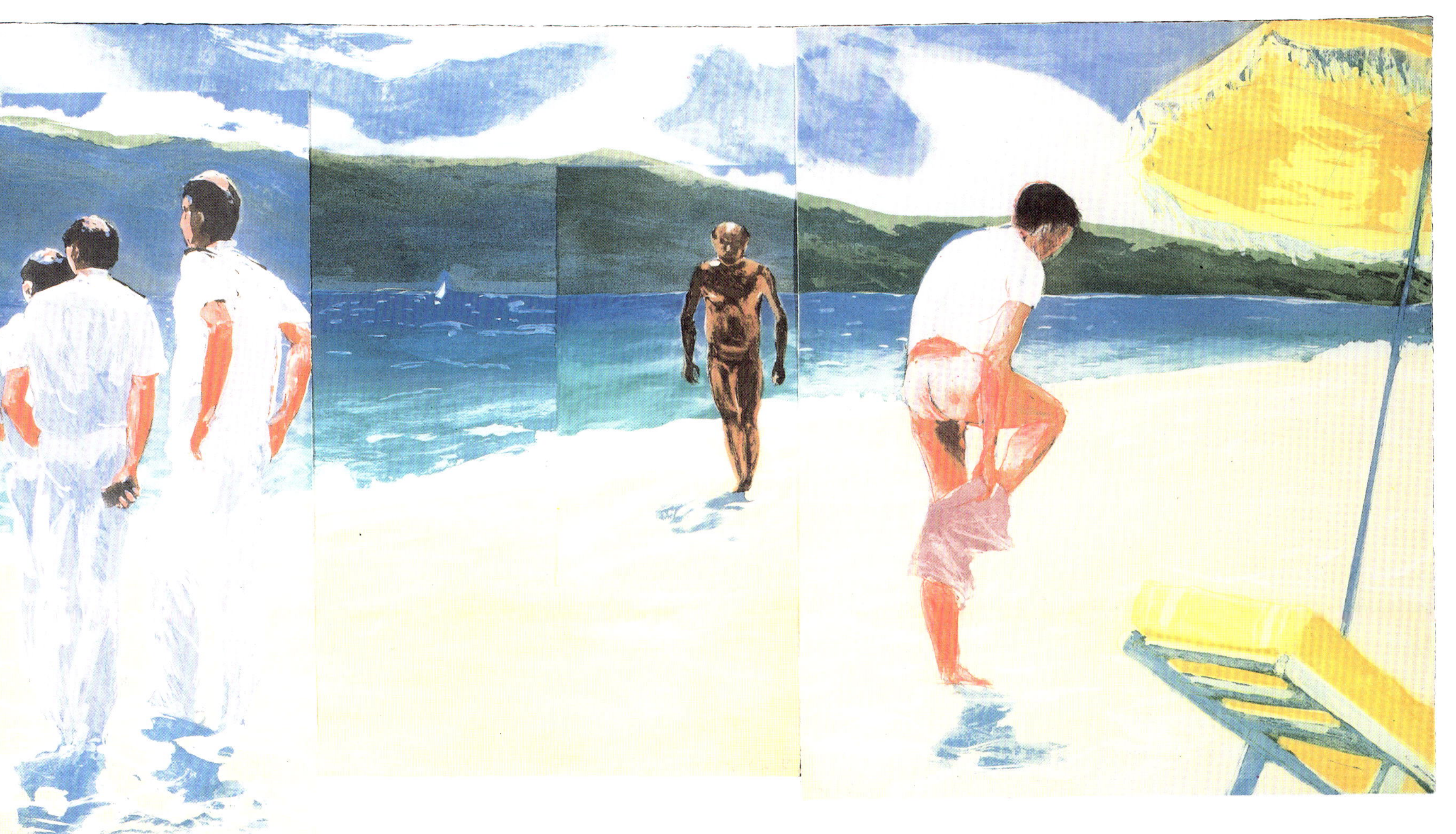

In 1977 Jörg Immendorff began a series of paintings, "Café Deutschland gut," followed several years later by a series of prints of the same subject. The café refers to the Rattinger Hof, a meeting place in Düsseldorf, and is used here as a forum for the artist's views about his homeland and its history. Using dynamic symbols, Immendorff depicts a divided and crippled Germany after World War II. The helmeted artist is seated in the foreground in the café, tearing a picture of Chairman Mao; behind him to the right is a mirrored column, juxtaposed with the Brandenburg Gate. At bottom is a broken red swastika, and sideways at the far right is a horse, part of the Roman Victory that once stood atop the Brandenburg Gate.

A remarkable relief print the size of a history painting, *Cities of Motion, Berlin* reinforces its thematic complexity through its ambitious composition. To accentuate the theme of conflict, Immendorff presents the symbols in a confrontational and chaotic manner reminiscent of a barroom brawl. Drab greens and grays reinforce the embattled appearance by evoking the colors of war, while the colorful splashes of paint intensify the pictorial turbulence and the artist's feeling of outrage.

Cities of Motion, Berlin, from the
"Café Deutschland gut" series
1983
Color linocut with hand coloring;
printed by the artist and assistants,
Düsseldorf; published by Maximilian
Verlag and Sabine Knust, Munich
69¾ x 90¼" (177.2 x 229.3 cm) sheet
1985-40-1

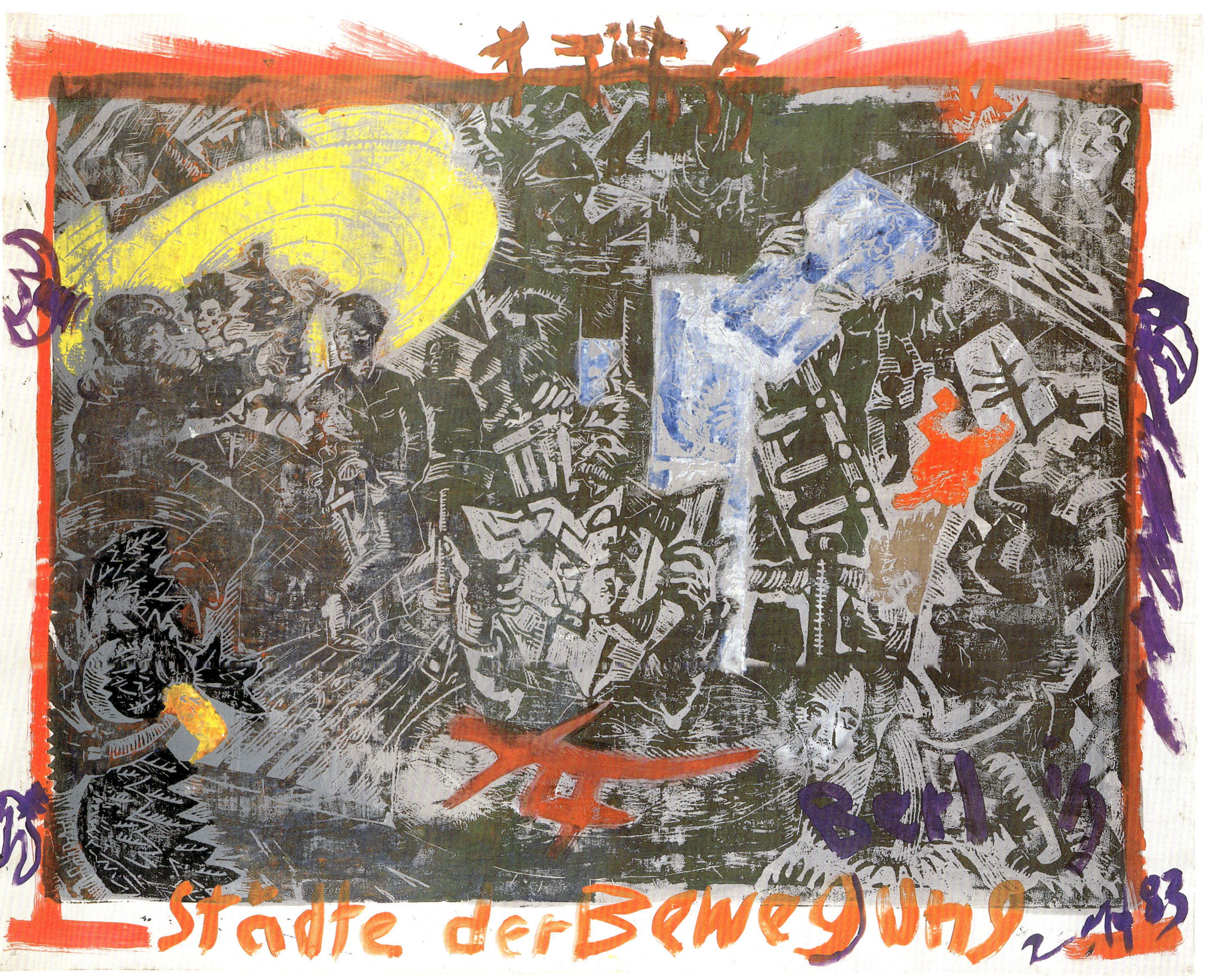

Städte der Bewegung
Berl
83

In her appropriation of subject matter from the mass media, Barbara Kruger typically begins with found material culled from magazines, movies, photographic annuals, or advertising. Here, however, she utilized nine still shots made in her studio. She enlarged, trimmed, and altered these images to transform her commonplace subjects into theatrical representations, and then superimposed an invented and ironic aphorism in bold type on its surface. The arresting visual effect is enhanced further by incorporating the viewer into the picture with the use of the personal pronoun: "*We* will no longer be seen and not heard." The urgency of the message reflects Kruger's successful use of the power of language to expose society's clichés, stereotypes, and power structures.

BARBARA **KRUGER**

Untitled
1985
Nine color lithographs with photo plates, hand-drawn plates, and silk-screen on Arches 88 paper; Arabic edition 50, Roman edition 10; printed by Maurice Sanchez and assistants at Derrière l'Etoile Studios, New York; published by Peter Blum Edition, New York
20½ x 20½" (52 x 52 cm) sheets
1986-131-1–9

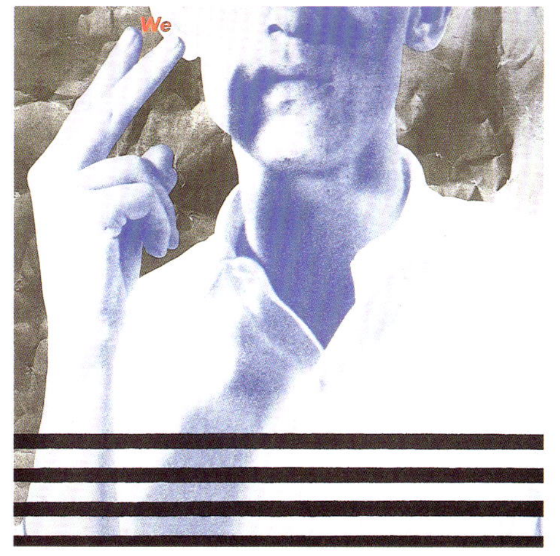
We
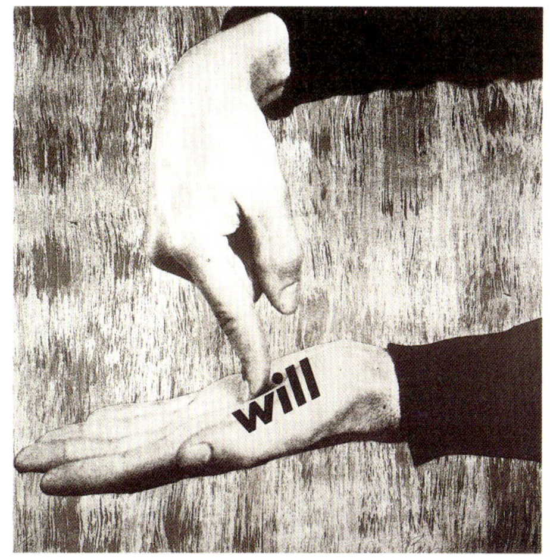
will
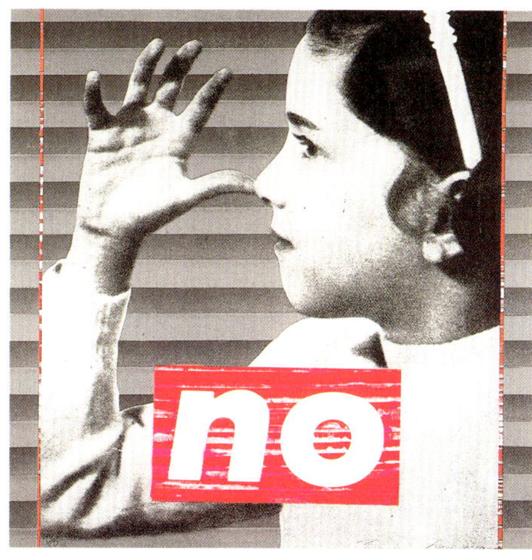
no
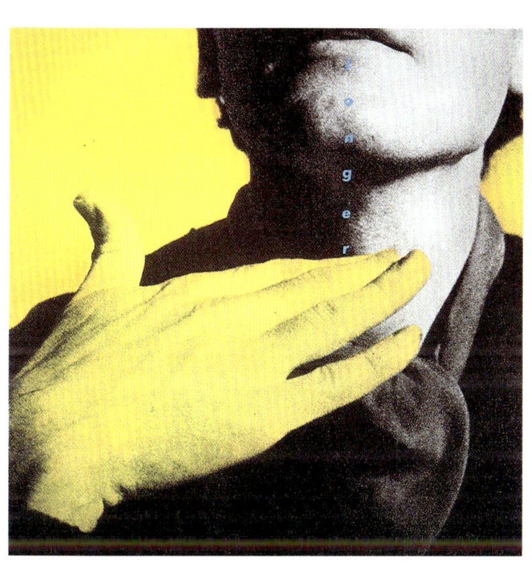
longer
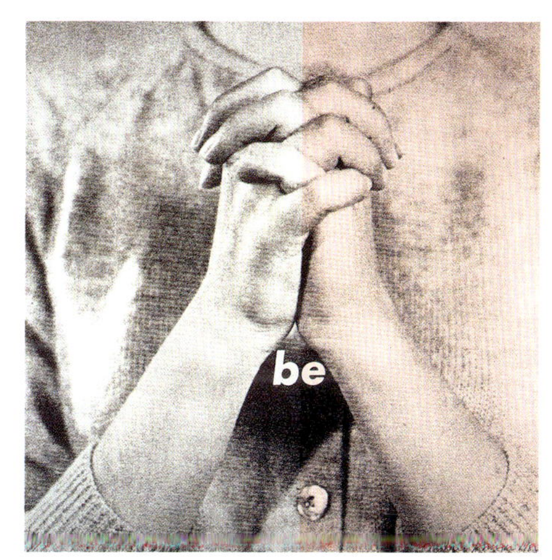
be
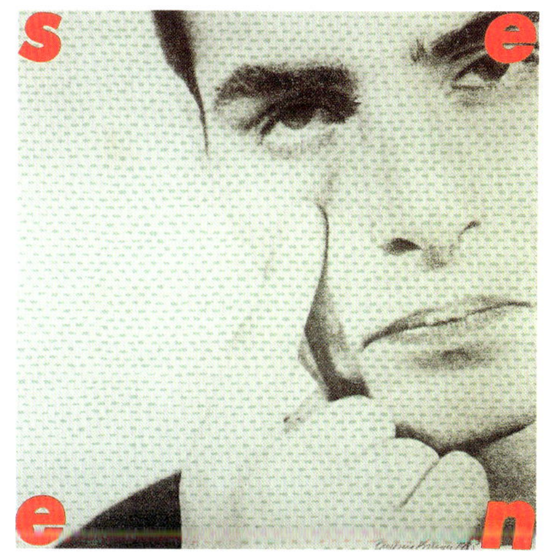
seen
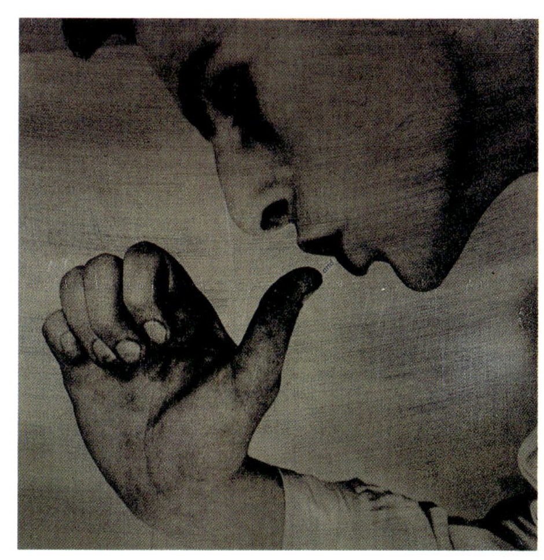
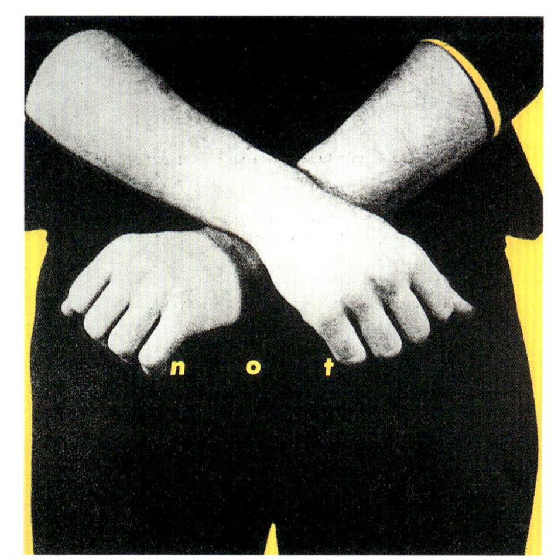
not
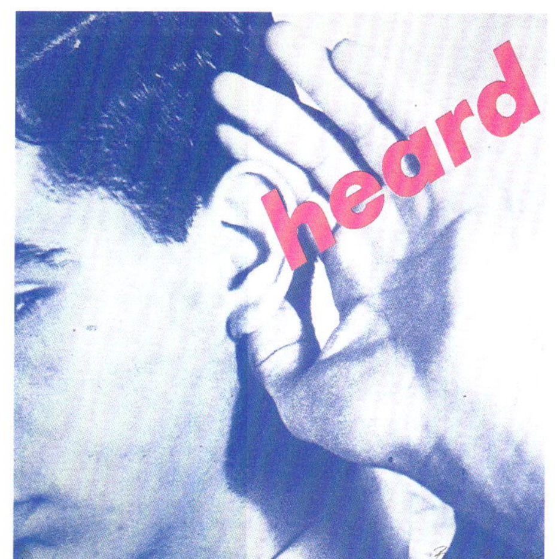
heard

Richard Long's works combine austere intellectual and conceptual premises with a highly romantic and English sense of place, a rootedness in nature and the landscape. His pieces are created primarily out-of-doors and throughout the world, from Ireland to Bolivia to Nepal, in the form of walks he takes from one place to another, often displacing stones, earth, or grass along the way to create elementary linear or circular configurations on the earth's surface. These are slow works, bound by the natural restraints of time, distance, and terrain. Their materials are physically real: mountains, deserts, trees, sky, stones, grass, flowers. The works take a second, more enduring physical form through the artist's production of photographs of landscapes with the configurations he has made, maps marked with the duration and parameters of his walks, word pieces in which words or phrases are arranged in shapes on sheets of paper, sticks or stones placed on floors in circular or linear configurations, and drawings with mud or muddy water on walls and, recently, on sheets of paper. Although these images may initially seem austere, they are charged with a high degree of sensuous impact.

Long's large-scale mud-circle drawings on paper are executed in mud with his hands or feet, and, of all his works convey the most vivid sense of his physical presence. The use of mud—earth and water combined, both of which Long employs extensively as materials—reflects the artist's profound interest in the surface of the earth and the passage of the footprints around and around on the sheet of paper evokes his long walks outdoors. Here the dense, opaque brown mud from the River Avon and its tendency to pool and splatter in places create an impression of turbulent, emotional intensity.

Mud Foot Circles
1985
Mud on paper laid on board
76⅜ x 87½" (194 x 222 cm)
1987-14-1

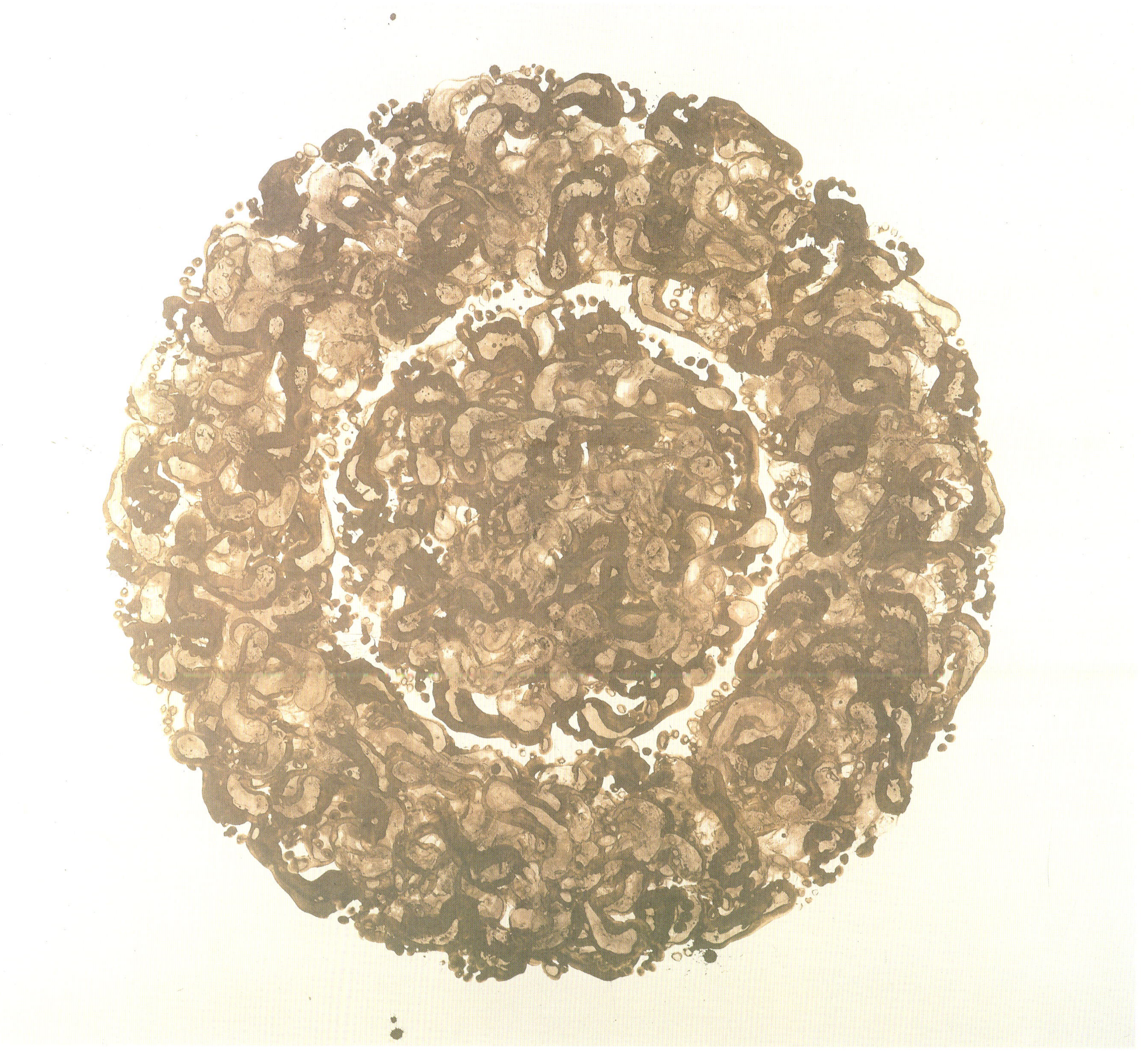

Before the destructive earthquake of 1980 in Naples, Nino Longobardi was working in a more or less conceptual manner, exhibiting room installations of draped and wrapped lengths of canvas and highly colored oil paintings with objects attached. After the earthquake, which destroyed his home and studio, his style changed drastically; he began to use a monochromatic palette, and his subjects took on a new emphasis of imagery and figuration. As in this drawing, he frequently combines charcoal and heavily worked gesso to create turbulent, visceral surfaces. His images—nudes, skulls, bones, skeletons, and animals— are ambivalently erotic or violent, and his stated admiration for the paintings of Goya, Turner, Van Gogh, and Francis Bacon is evident in his emotionally charged handling of his materials.

Longobardi is a native Neapolitan, and the character of Naples permeates his art. Wedged, in Goethe's phrase, between God and the devil, the city today nourishes an ancient, dark, and primitive side; over the centuries a continual succession of violent events such as plagues, earthquakes, and volcanic eruptions have disrupted life in this region of sublime natural beauty. Longobardi's images reflect a similar ambivalence between the threatening or catastrophic and the beautiful and seductive. He has said that he is interested in painting that is free of any set definition of style, beauty, or finish. In Longobardi's words, "Death is always present in life. If I just wanted to sell things, I'd paint flowers. I think art is more than beauty—for me, it is something with multi-layered imagery, not always so palatable."*

* *The Print Collector's Newsletter*, vol. 15, no. 3 (July– August 1984), p. 105.

Untitled
1983
Gesso, charcoal, and wash on three pieces of paper
30½ x 66″ (77.5 x 167.7 cm) assembled
1984-74-1

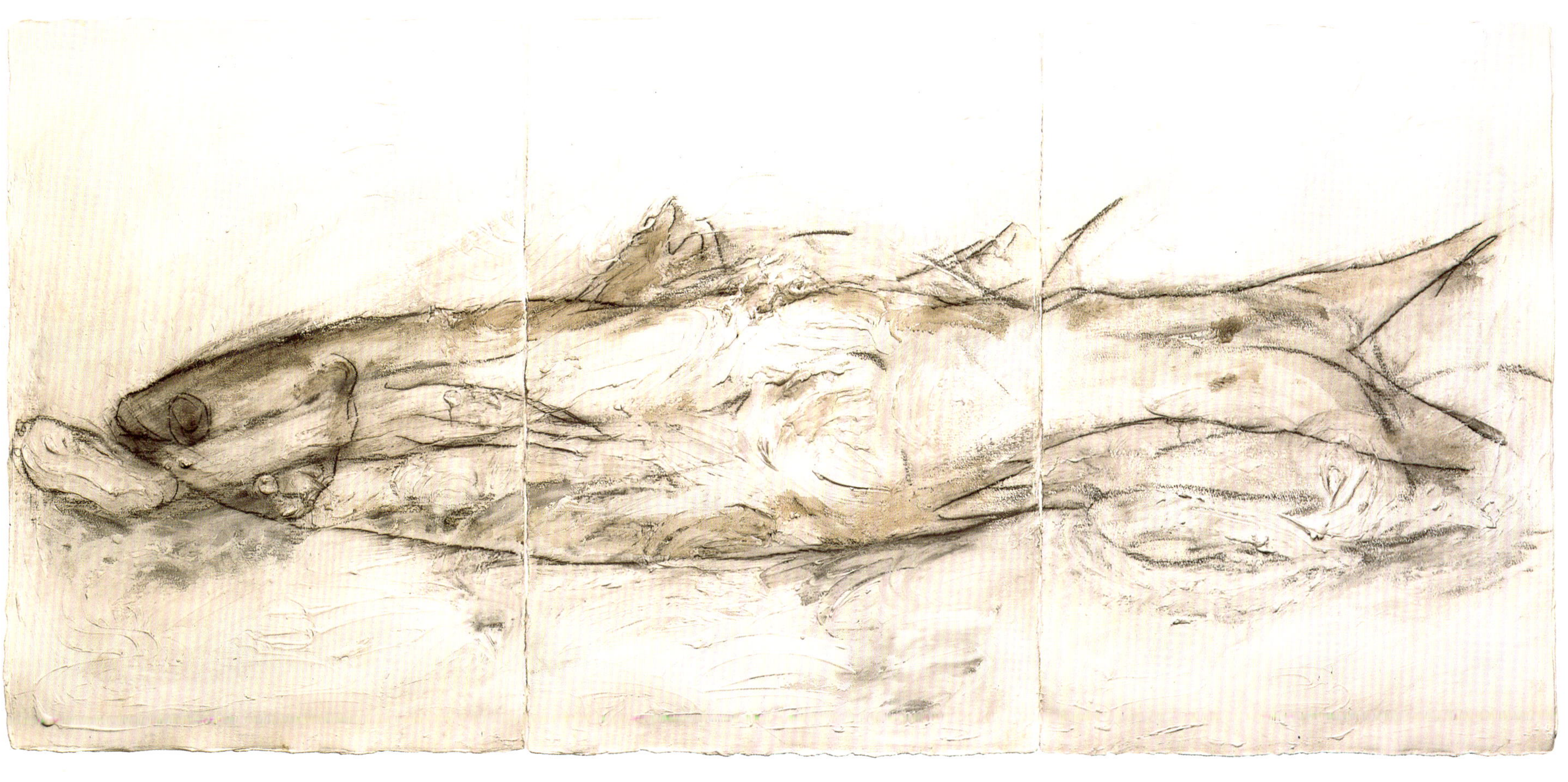

Although Elizabeth Murray can be regarded as an Abstract painter, her images are almost always grounded in some literal shape—usually a household object such as a cup, telephone, shoe, or table, and in this case, a paintbrush—that she reads in different visual ways, blurring the line between abstract form and recognizable image. Her art has evolved slowly from a Chicago funk, fantasy-oriented figural style in the late 1960s to her current abstract manner developed in the mid 1970s. Working in New York since 1967, she has consistently addressed the issue of painting during a time when Minimal and Conceptual concerns served for many artists to deemphasize the power of the object and the act of painting itself.

In 1980, when *Second Painter's Partner* was done, Murray was beginning to explore the formal device of shattering and reunifying images in both drawings and paintings, the former executed on several pieces of cut or torn paper assembled in eccentric configurations, and the latter on fragmented pieces of shaped canvas conjoined like loosely assembled picture puzzles. Murray seeks to show the slow emergence of her images from layer after layer of color, worked up and rubbed down in the drawings, erased and built up again, so that ghosts of previous designs remain. She sets up certain tensions in the idea of disintegration versus coherence through fragmented but unified images; at the same time she is intensely involved with the sensual, physical properties of her medium and with the subjective, emotional potential of shapes and colors. Layers of densely worked pastel tones—green over pink over orange over white, black over blue over orange over mauve—build up the image in this drawing. The pigment is applied in streaks, smudges, jabs, and swirls that infuse the work with energy and a sense of emotional tension.

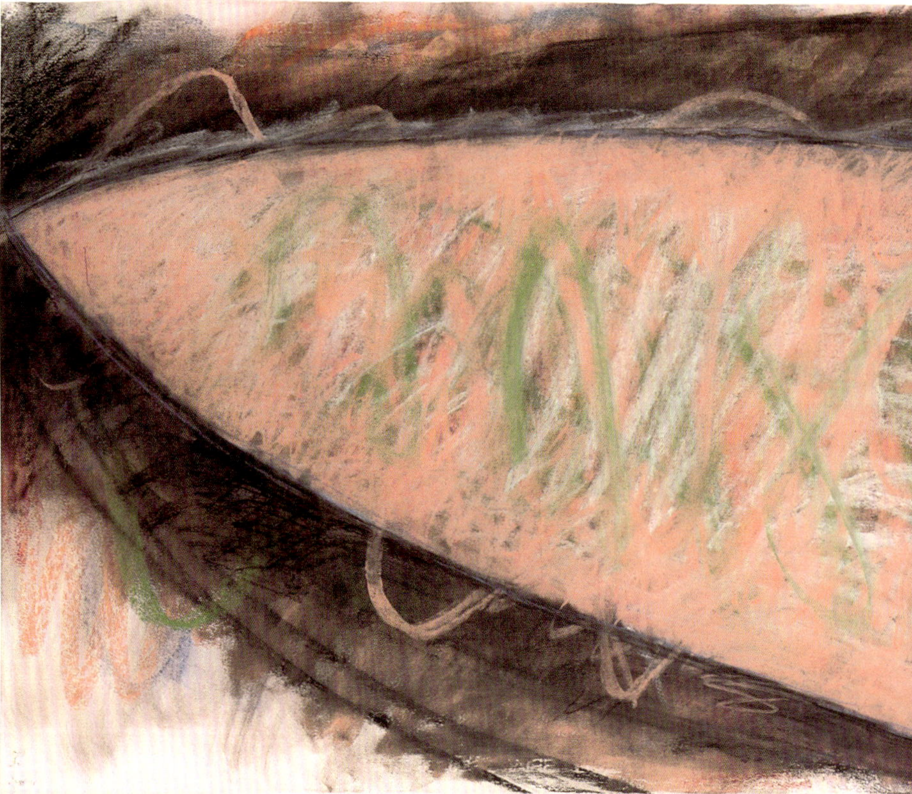

Second Painter's Partner
1980
Pastel on three pieces of Fabriano CMF
wove paper
29 x 85⅜" (73.6 x 216.9 cm) assembled
1981-17-1

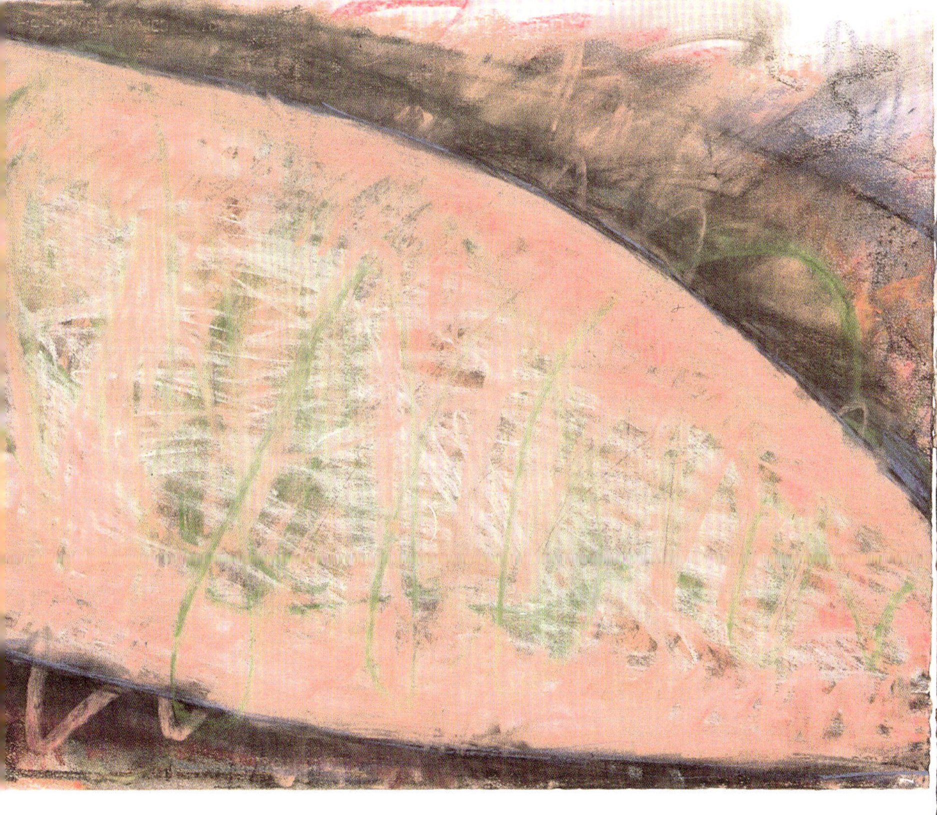
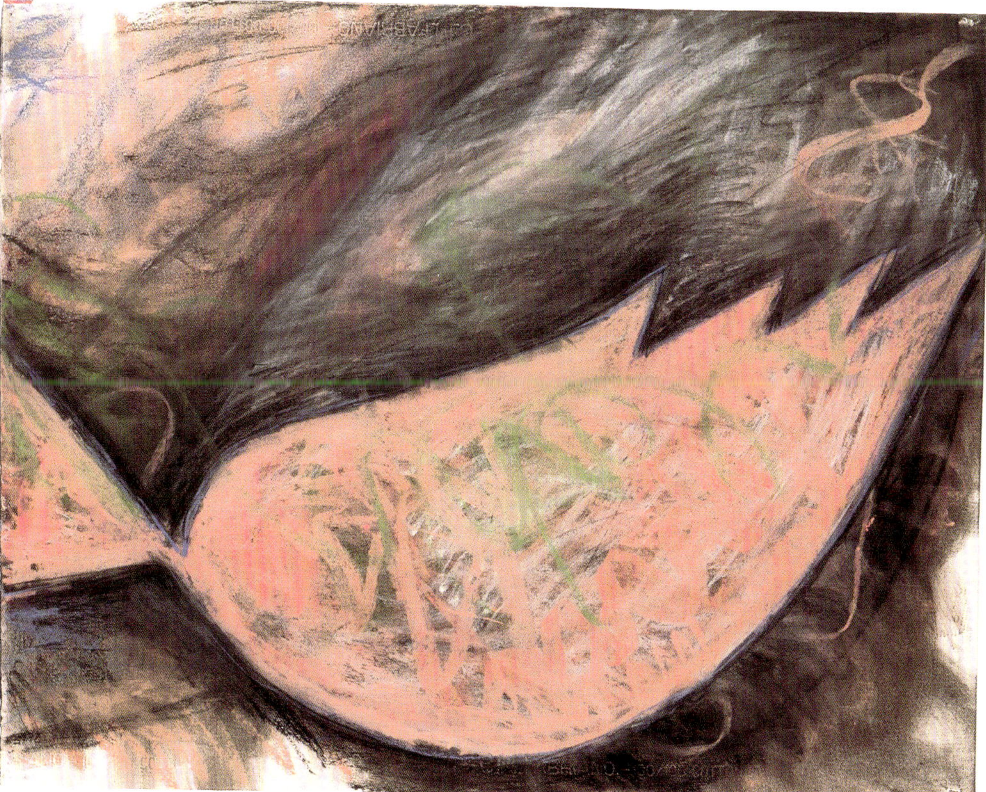

Dennis Oppenheim's work has evolved through an intensely varied sequence of primarily Conceptual modes since he began exhibiting in the late 1960s. Until 1977 the works he produced were more or less transitory and nonmaterial, supporting an anticommodity approach to art; these included large-scale, site-related earthworks—shifting, transporting, or otherwise marking soil, crops, or snow—or small-scale "body" art—using his own body as an expressive tool or sculptural material—or gallery installations using mannequins or puppets. In 1977 his work began to move into a more constructive idiom with the emergence of his "machineworks," for which he is primarily known today. These elegant constructions of industrial elements and materials—steel, fiberglass, rubber, conveyor belts, motors, pulleys, cables, and so forth—are often accompanied by large drawings in graphite and colored pencil or wash.

. . . And the Mind Grew Fingers, in which with a richly sensuous combination of mediums, the artist produces an energetic and colorful explosion of swirling lines and splatters of wash, marks a point in Oppenheim's work when his machine pieces often assumed anatomical shapes—heads, hands, or rib cages—as opposed to abstract, mechanical ones. Several versions and variations of projects are related to this image of a topless, exploding head: for example, a twenty-four-foot-high steel and aluminum sculpture produced for Artpark in Lewiston, New York, in 1984, in which fireworks were ignited within a head-shaped armature, and a recent unexecuted proposal for the Charlottenburg Gate in West Berlin, which introduces a huge fan to wave a number of ribbon-like, fiberglass streamers attached to a thirteen-foot-high steel head. Oppenheim finds the working of machines an apt metaphor for the working of the human mind: "The factory becomes the mind; what is produced or what enters this structure becomes *thought*. The process of thought is thus preserved and integrated into the work after its construction, rather than being consumed in its production."* This drawing is a particular metaphor for the creative process of drawing for the artist. As he remarked in a 1984 interview about machine works as a kind of drawing, "more and more, I realized that the drawing really comes from the fingers. It's as if the mind has grown fingers."†

. . . And the Mind Grew Fingers
1984
Graphite, crayon, ink, charcoal, oil wash, and oil pastel on wove paper
50⅛ x 38¼" (127.3 x 97.2 cm)
1984-46-1

* Quoted by Anne L. Munroe in the exhibition brochure accompanying "Dennis Oppenheim," San Francisco Museum of Modern Art (May 3–June 10, 1984), n.p.

† Alain G. Joyaux, *Dennis Oppenheim: Accelerator for Evil Thoughts* (Muncie, Indiana, 1985), p. 18.

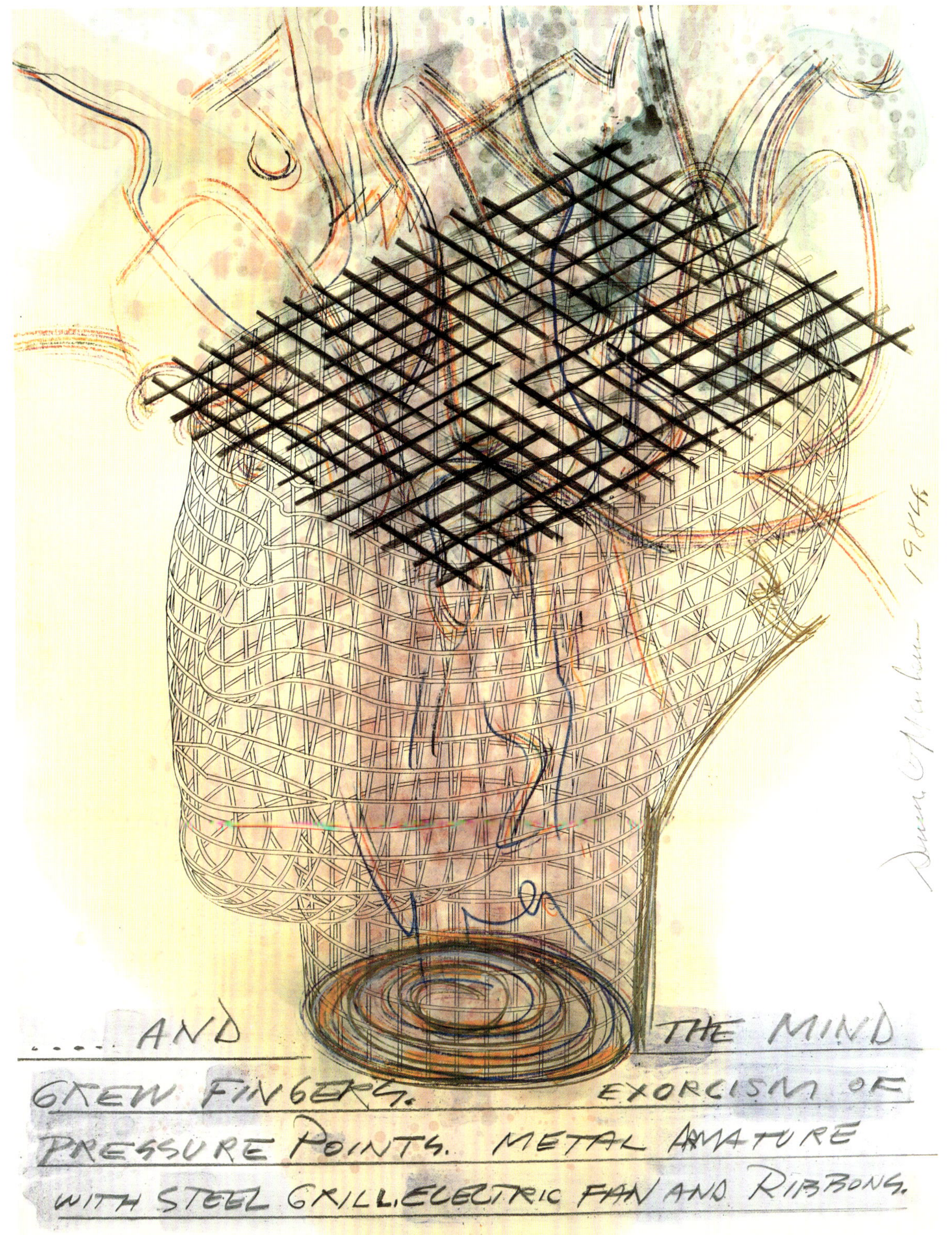

.... AND   THE MIND
GREW FINGERS.   EXORCISM OF
PRESSURE POINTS. METAL ARMATURE
WITH STEEL GRILL, ELECTRIC FAN AND RIBBONS.

Howardena Pindell works on paper and canvas, as well as in the medium of "video drawings." In the early 1970s she was drawing or spraying dots onto canvas through templates of patterns punched in sheets of paper. Then she began to accumulate and use the bits of paper punched from the templates, and by 1975 she was producing works with dozens of tiny discs, punched from paper painted with watercolor or gouache, loaded onto grids of thread, and attached with spray adhesive. These pieces grew increasingly three-dimensional and colorful; the series of 1977, to which this drawing belongs, is embellished with sequins, glitter, gold paint, and powdered pigment. The personal nature of these works is enhanced by the incorporation of collage fragments of postcards, notes, correspondence, and even bank checks belonging to the artist and by her use of handmade paper.

Although Pindell, who trained and matured as a black woman artist in a traditional, male-dominated art system in America of the 1960s, does not use specific female or feminist imagery, there is an underlying political aspect to her rejection of traditional materials of painting in favor of decorative, craftsman-like materials and modes of working. The preciousness and exuberance of this small work, with its constellations of brightly colored dots clumped and clustered along grids of thread, sparkling with a scattering of blue glitter, afford it a special place in the mode of pattern-oriented art of the late 1970s.

Untitled No. 89
1977
Acrylic, gouache, watercolor, thread, glitter, and cut paper on board
14⅜ x 10½" (36.5 x 26.7 cm)
1979-142-1

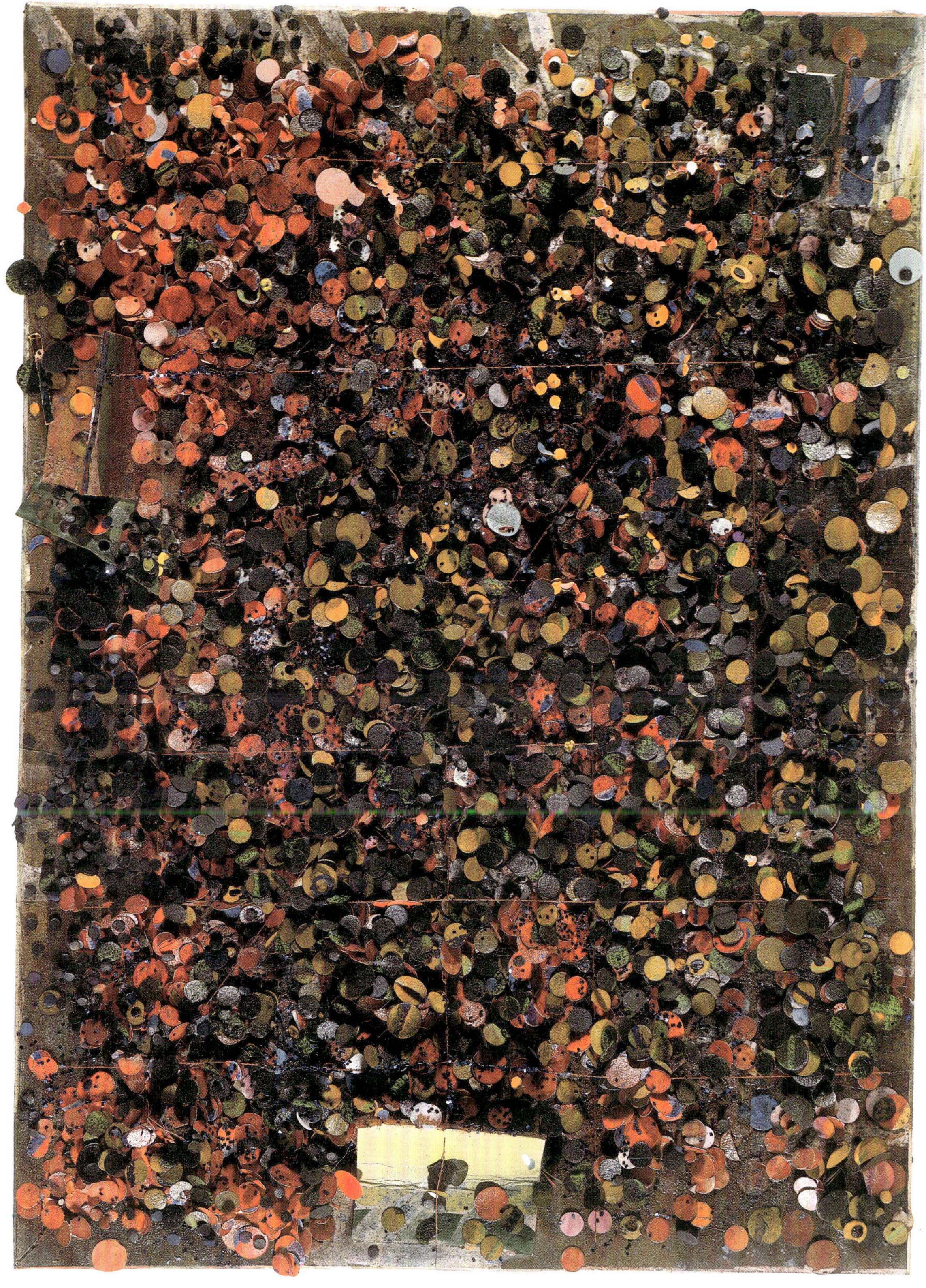

Since the mid 1970s Jody Pinto has been making site-specific installations—usually outdoors and constructed of "workingmen's" materials, such as concrete, bricks, timber, or cement blocks—for which parts of the body often serve as the architectural "root." For Pinto, the human body is the central source of information for everything we see, understand, and replicate. She expresses certain emotions or states of being by evoking particular parts of the body, which are also conflated with landscape elements in her art: Mouths gush forth rivers, a column of vertebrae forms a mountain range, and severed fingers become a set of hills. Hay is used in several of her early pieces to represent hair, which like grass exists above and below the surface of the body/earth and stands for anger, passion, or humor. Thus an architectural surface in one of Pinto's works will "bristle" with energy and become personified.

Split Tongue Pier is related to an outdoor installation executed for Swarthmore College in the fall of 1980, which was constructed of two planks of wood stretching out over a creek flanked by vertical beams like a dock, and to an indoor piece done for the Morris Gallery of the Pennsylvania Academy of the Fine Arts in the same year. Pinto's installation pieces are meant to be entered, traversed, or otherwise physically experienced. In the same way her watercolors are exceptionally physical objects, with poolings and puddlings of brilliant color applied with industrial paintbrushes (which hold a great deal of water) overlaid with exuberant, graphically bold strokes of crayon or graphite, or both. In *Split Tongue Pier* the fierce black jut of the tongue/pier looms against a hellish, fiery red-orange ground, a strange contrast to the serenity of the woodland setting of the work as it was eventually executed, which reflects the artist's fascination with the ambiguity existing between sensuousness and violence, tranquility and passion.

Split Tongue Pier
1980
Crayon, graphite, and watercolor on wove paper
39⅛ x 59″ (99.3 x 149.9 cm)
1981-19-1

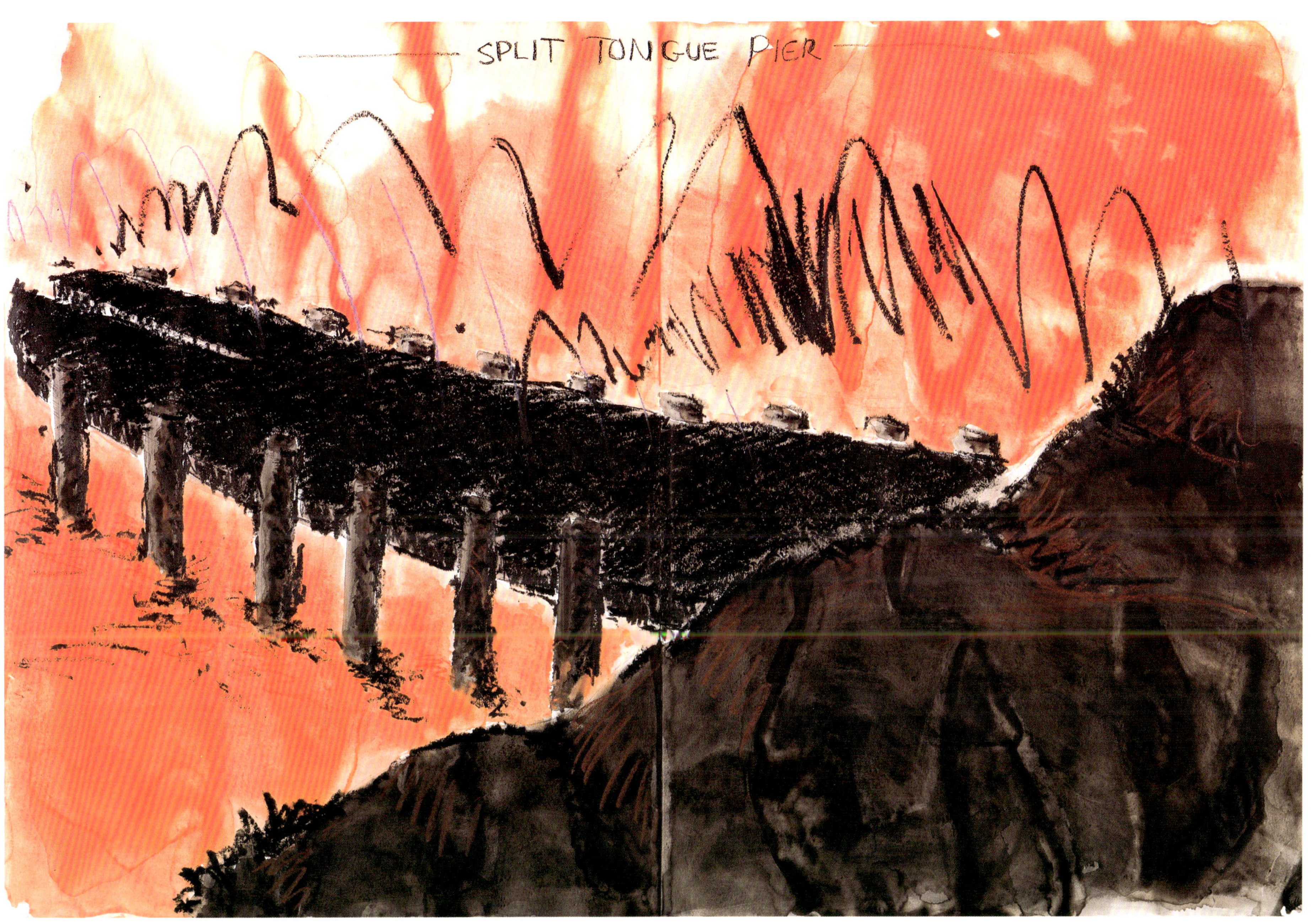
SPLIT TONGUE PIER

Susan Rothenberg's approach to her art is intuitive and improvisational, as she
has explained: "Most of my work is not seen through a rational part of my
brain. It comes from a place in me that I don't choose to examine. I just let it
come."* Two of her major influences are the isolated and attenuated sculptures
of Alberto Giacometti and the elemental subjects and gestural marks of Jasper
Johns. Rothenberg's compendium of distinctive images includes horses, heads
and hands, and boats, which as seen here, she transforms into abstract and
dreamlike forms that are difficult to comprehend. Are the figures emerging
from the sea,or are they flat on a velvety surface? Is the elongated diamond a
boat and its reflection, or is it a vaginal form? Is the ghostly figure protectively
embracing the boat, or does it hinder its passage? Typically, her images remain
ambiguous, but the artist has offered some explanation of the meaning of her
boat pictures: 'What I think the work was starting to talk about is growing,
taking journeys. The boat became a symbol to me—about the freedom I was
feeling."†

* Hayden Herrera, "Expressionism Today:
   An Artists' Symposium," *Art in America*,
   vol. 70, no. 11 (December 1982), p. 65.
† Ibid., pp. 65 ff.

SUSAN **ROTHENBERG**

Untitled
1983
Drypoint, aquatint, burnishing, and
etching on Somerset Satin paper; edition
35 and 9 proofs; printed (by Charles
Levine) and published at Mountain
Shadow Studio, Highland, New York
25½ x 21⅝" (63.5 x 54.9 cm) plate
1984-10-1

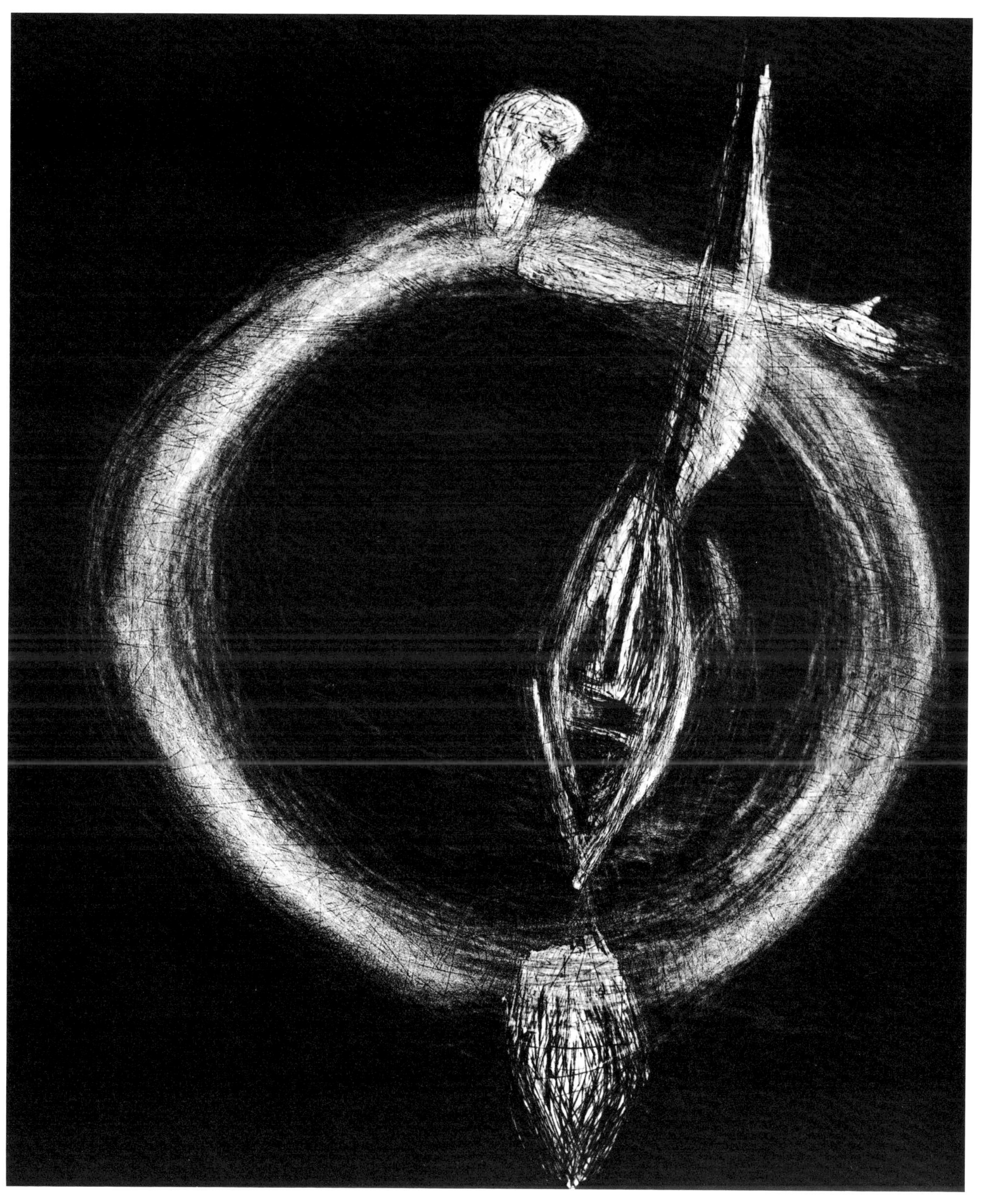

Since the early 1970s Joel Shapiro has worked simultaneously as a sculptor
and draftsman. In each medium he has explored the complex problem of forms
and their spatial relationships in separate and very different ways. His iron or
bronze sculptures are simplified images of objects, such as houses, chairs, or
tables, and of human figures reduced to the proportions of stick figures. In his
drawings, Shapiro's concerns are also worked out in simple, abstract, geometric
forms, which link his work visually and conceptually with Minimal art of the
1960s. Yet he insists upon deviating from purely formal concerns: The
smudges, erasures, and unconcealed changes in his drawings suggest his more
personal, even emotional, involvement in the issues of form and space. The
austere, analytical, and dogmatic character of Minimal art is eschewed in this
powerful, yet paradoxically intimate, drawing of 1981.

Ambiguity and multiple, shifting solutions to problems are the essential
elements of Shapiro's forceful images. The apparently straightforward relationships of black to white, the intersections of ruled lines, and the resulting clear
shapes are charged with infinite dualities. For example, the dense charcoal bars
can be read individually or traced as a continuous line, and even as erasures
and smudges create a sense of atmosphere, the artist's fingerprints mark the
paper's impenetrable surface.

JOEL **SHAPIRO**

Untitled
1981
Charcoal on wove paper
32⅛ x 39¾″ (81.6 x 101.1 cm)
1982-8-1

Robert Wilson views his plays as a succession of tableaux and the print medium
as a kind of theatrical production. In this portfolio he represents scenes from
Wagner's opera *Parsifal*. "The difference between Wagner and me," Wilson
says, "is that his visuals are always subservient to the text—reinforce the text—
and I think the visual is what I see."*

Each of the nineteen prints in the series is based on the theme of water and
is presented with simple and direct images constituting a unified entity, consist-
ing of actors, objects, time, light, and space.

In the first image, instead of a stage curtain there is what Wilson calls a
curtain of light. In the second and third images, Gurnemanz, the knight of the
Holy Grail, appears as an incidental spot and then slowly fades away. In the
fifth and sixth, a great disc of light and an iceberg float across the stage, and in
the tenth, light seems to glow through a veil.

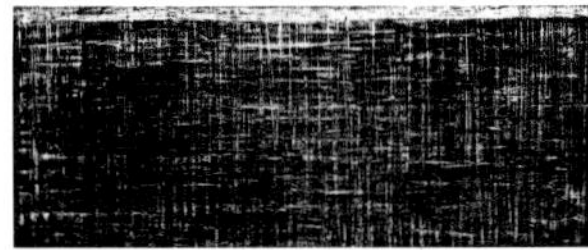

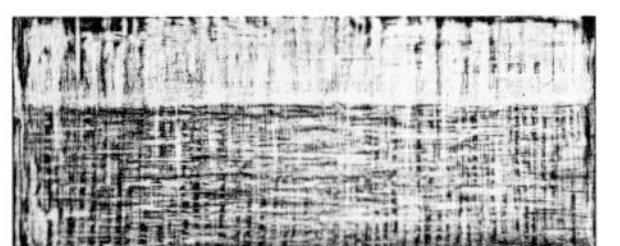

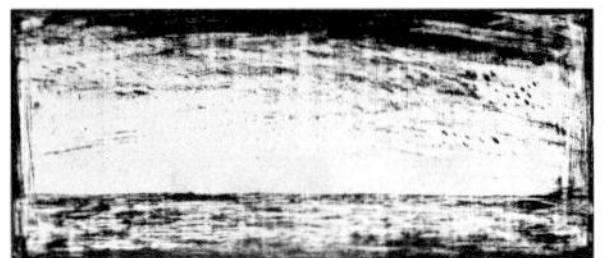

a

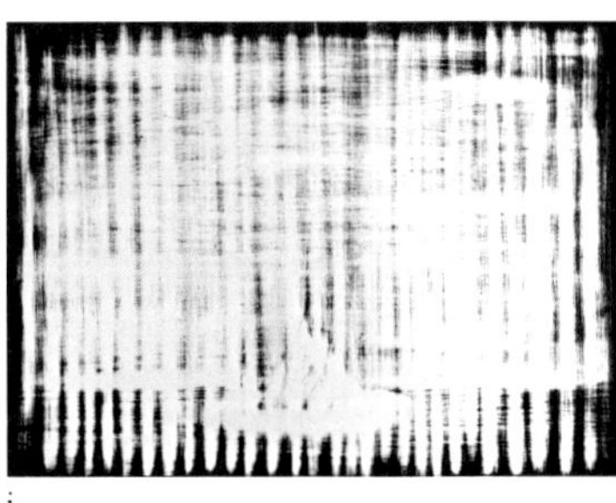

j

Parsifal
1985
Nineteen lithographs on various types
and sizes of paper; edition 35; printed
by Karl Imhof, Munich; published by
Fred Jahn, Munich
1986-74-1a–s

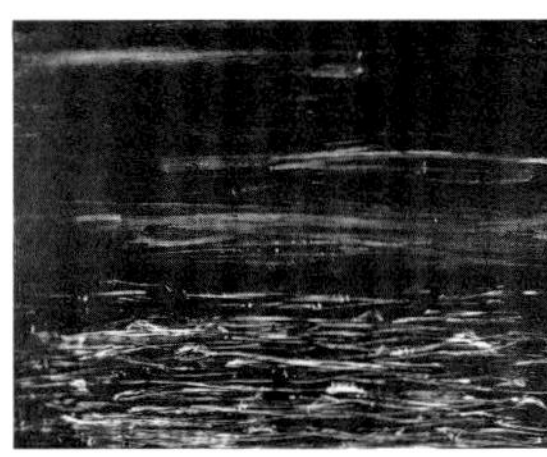

o

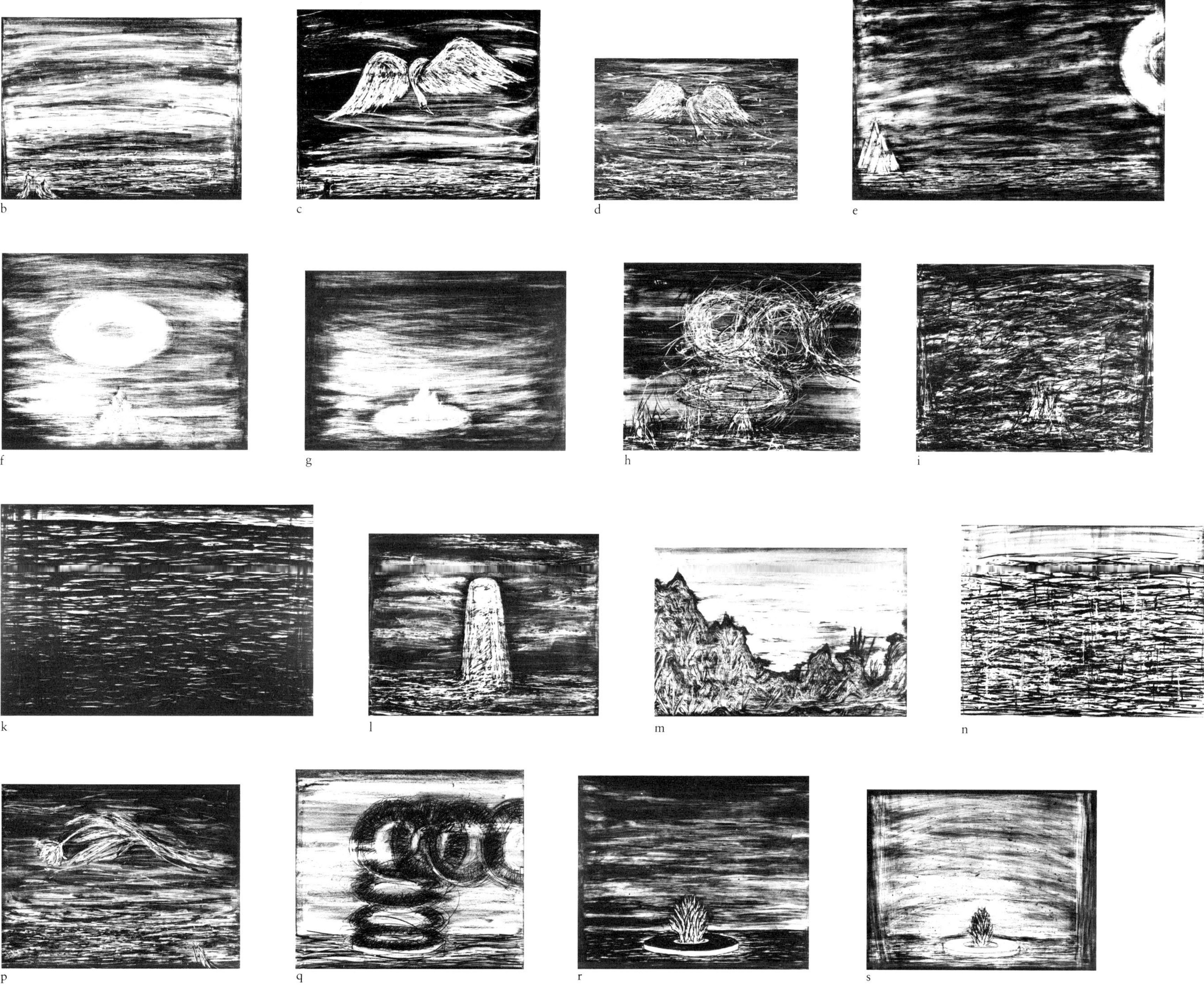

b

c

d

e

f

g

h

i

k

l

m

n

p

q

r

s

Terry Winters's organic forms derive from morphological observations. As if under a microscope, the morula, or cell images, appear in various manifestations—porous and reticular, dense and amorphous, delicate and crystalline—and grow, collide, and multiply. The extreme enlargement of the organisms tends to diminish their representational character, however, enhancing their abstract appearance, and they appear strange, like foreign bodies inexplicably drifting into our perceptual field. Winters's elaborate manipulation of the surface with smudges, erasures, and reworked passages draws attention to the process of art, the real subject of these works. In turn, the skillful treatment of the lithographic medium may be seen as a metaphor for Winters's critical examination of the living organism.

Morula I, II, and III
1983–84
Three color lithographs on handmade Toyoshi paper; editions 38, 37, and 36; printed (by Thomas Cox and Keith Brintzenhofe) and published at Universal Limited Art Editions, West Islip, New York
42 x 32″ (106.8 x 81 cm), 42¾ x 32⅜″ (108.5 x 82.2 cm), 42¾ x 32⅜″ (108.5 x 82.3 cm) sheets
1984-48-1–3

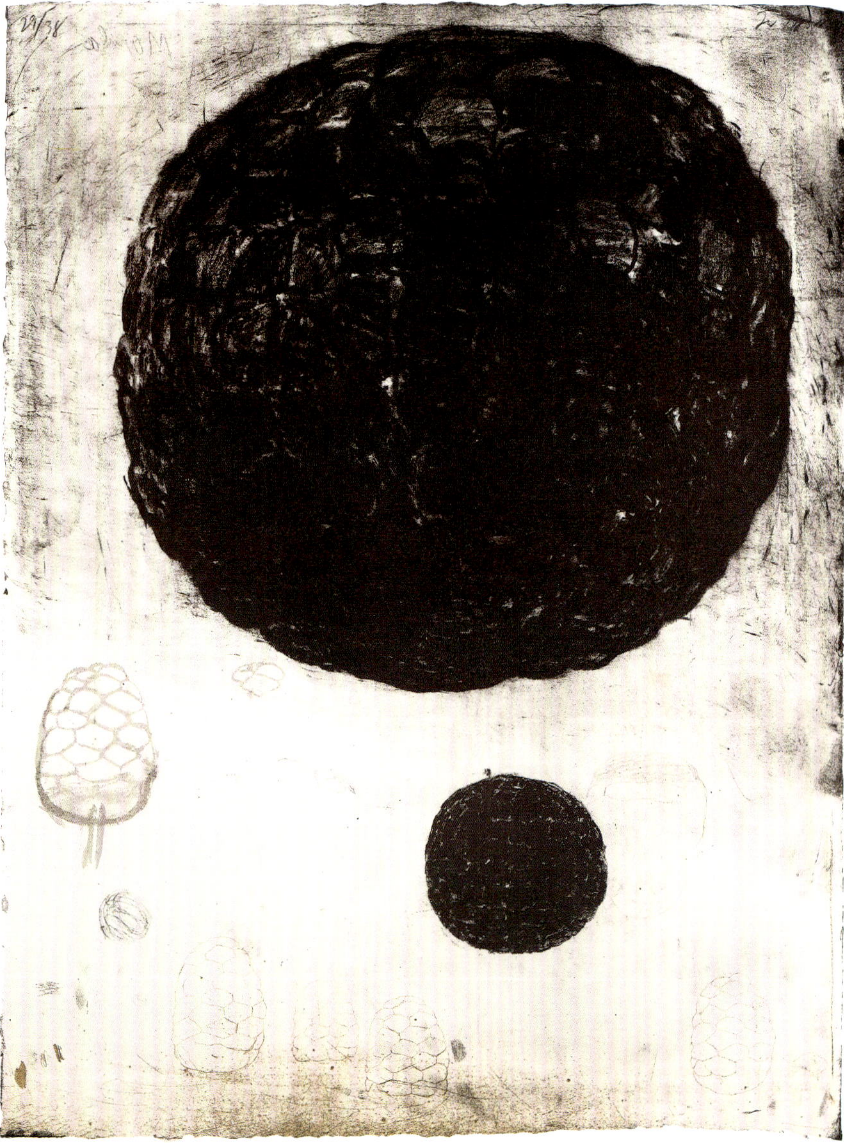

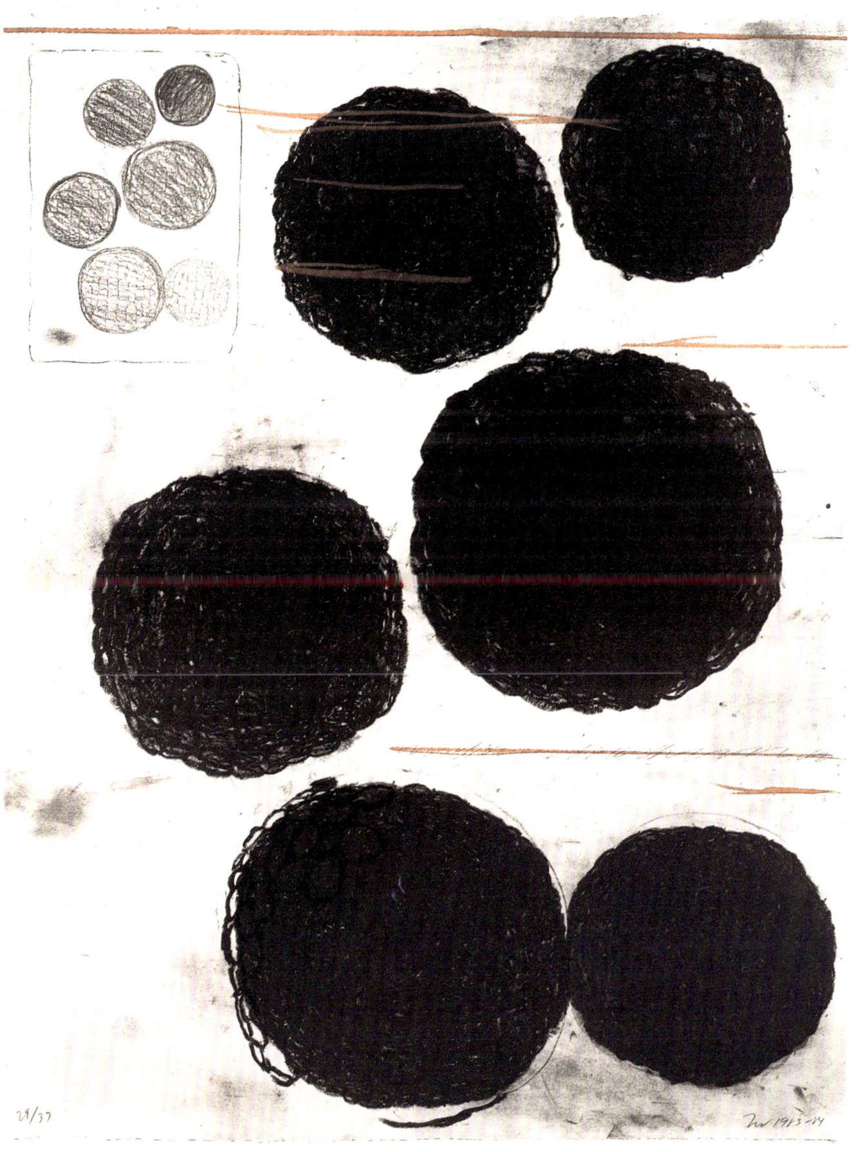
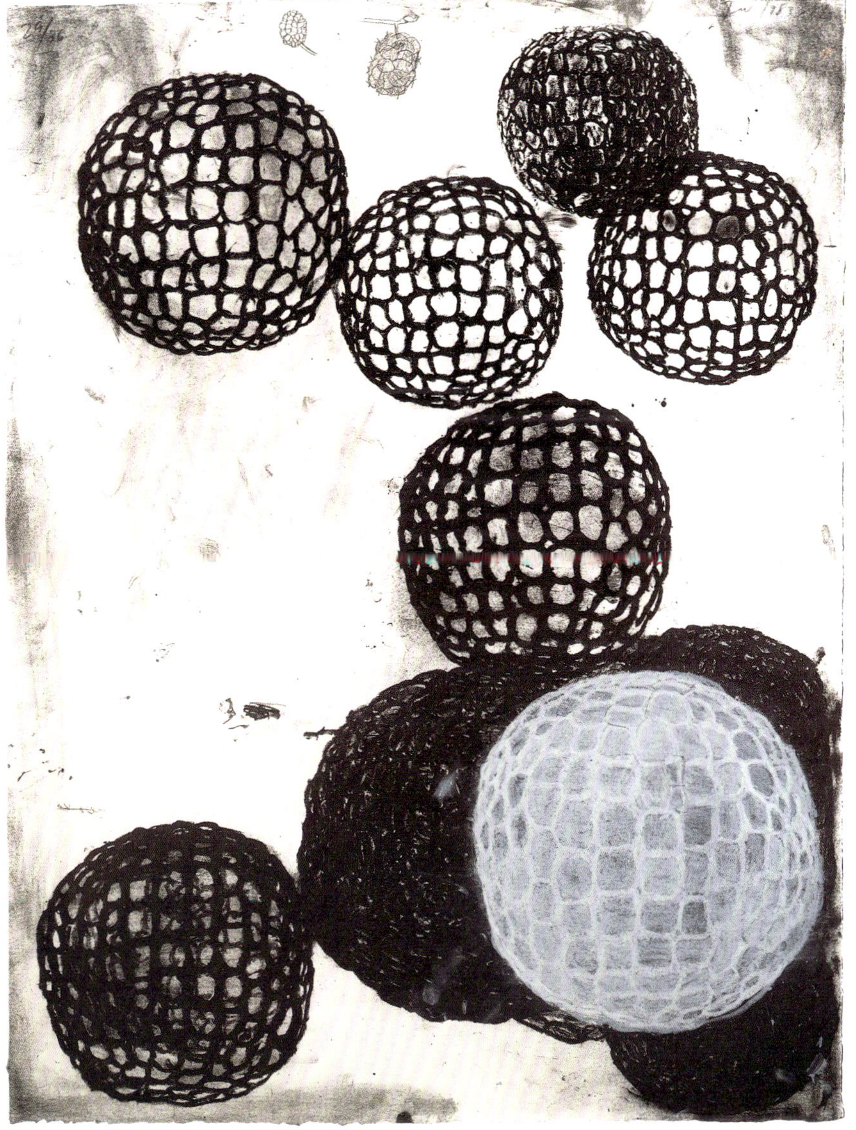

Robert Zakanitch is associated with a group of printmakers who explore paper
as a medium in itself, such as in this work, which was made of colored paper
pulp, formed in molds and then pressed and dried. The tactile surface, which
seems to engender the blossoming flowers, is but one example of the harmony
of form and content that characterizes Zakanitch's oeuvre. Coming from a
background that stressed such styles as Abstract Expressionism and
Minimalism, Zakanitch turned in the 1970s to pattern and decoration as his
subject matter, a mode that emphasized the aspects of beauty and lush physical-
ity seen in *Double Peacock No. 2*.

ROBERT **ZAKANITCH**

Double Peacock No. 2
1981
Colored and pressed paper pulp, and
watercolor; printed at Tyler Graphics
Ltd., Mount Kisco, New York
49 x 36⅛″ (124.3 x 91.6 cm) sheet
1981-61-1

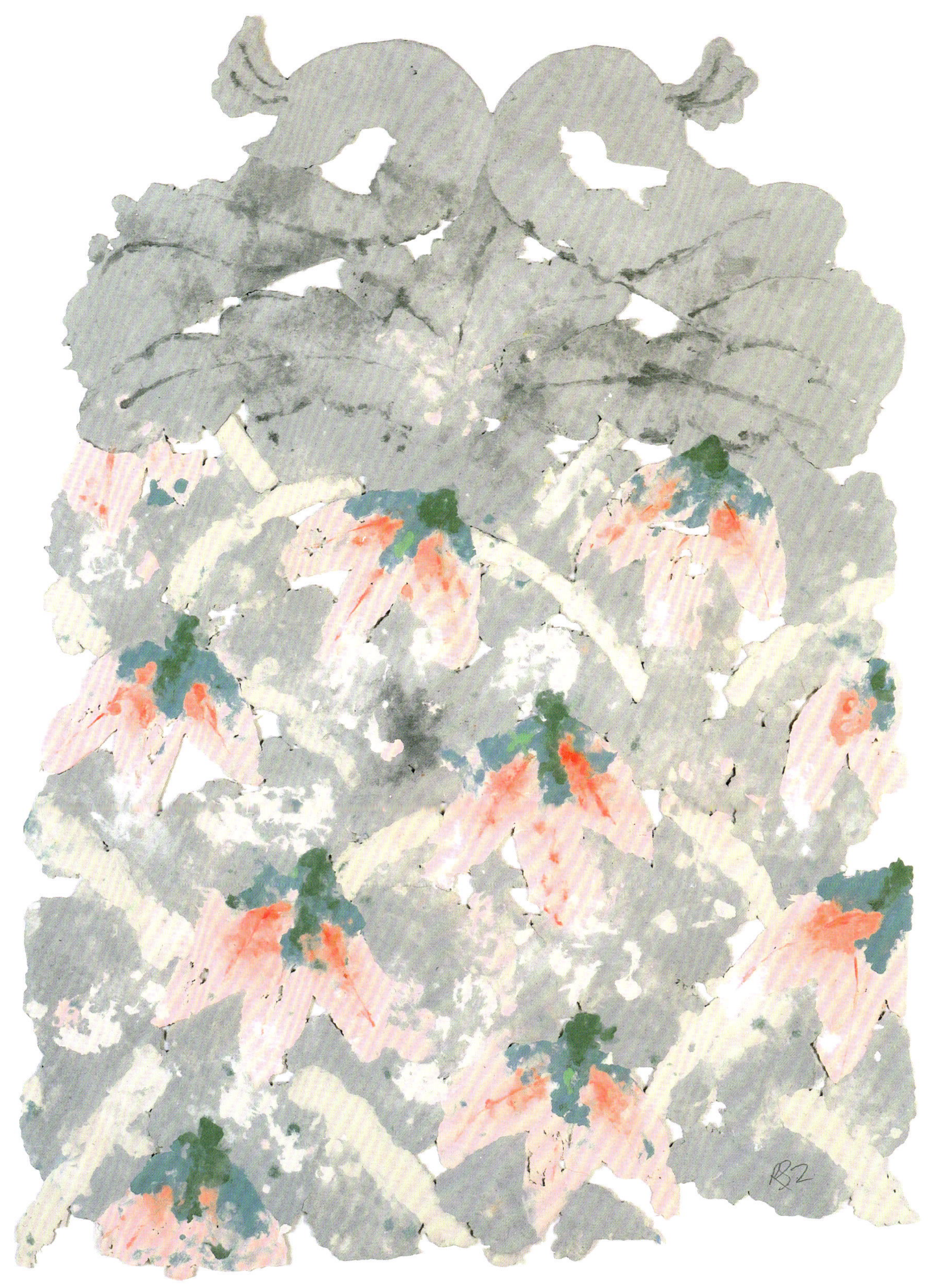

Checklist of the Collection and Biographies of the Artists

Works illustrated with Plates are not
reproduced in the Checklist

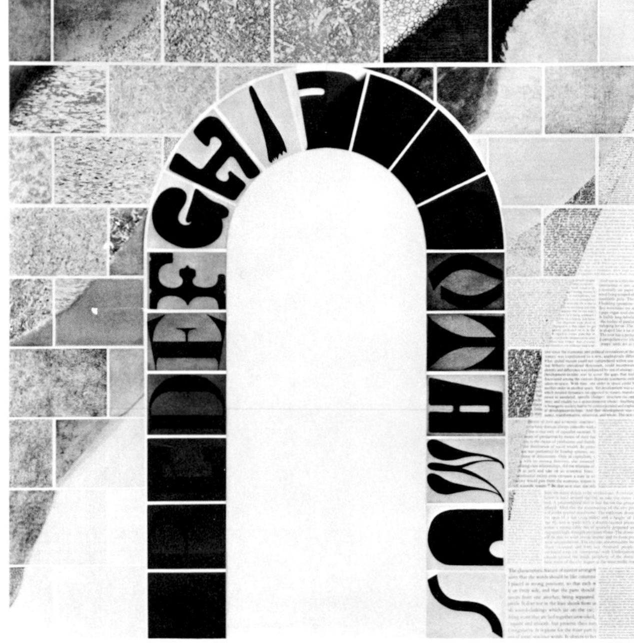

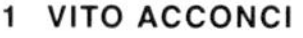

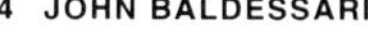

7

1 VITO ACCONCI

Born 1940, Bronx, New York
Studied Holy Cross College, Worcester,
Massachusetts, B.A. 1962
University of Iowa, M.F.A. 1964
Teaches Parsons School of Design, New
York
Resides Brooklyn

Vito Acconci works in a variety of mediums,
including performance, photography, video,
film, and installation. Since his first solo
exhibition at the Rhode Island School of
Design, Providence, in 1969, he has become
an influential and widely exhibited artist.
Retrospective exhibitions were held at the
Stedelijk Museum, Amsterdam, in 1978 and
at the Museum of Contemporary Art,
Chicago, in 1980. Acconci's prints have
been included in numerous group exhibitions in the United States, notably the National Print Exhibition (1986) at The Brooklyn Museum. He has also shown in "Documenta" (1972, 1982) in Kassel, West
Germany, and in the Venice Biennale (1976,
1978, 1980).

Reference La Jolla Museum of Contemporary Art, California. *Vito Acconci: Domestic
Trappings*. June 5–August 2, 1987.

Building-Blocks for a Doorway
1983–85
Photoetching, hard ground, soft ground,
and aquatint in four colors, from 62 plates
on two pieces of Arches Cover paper; 8
numbered edition and 8 proofs; photowork
by George Holzer; published by
Graphicstudio, University of South Florida
93⅞ x 94½" (238.4 x 240 cm) assembled
1988-2-1

2 ROBERT ARNESON

Born 1930, Benicia, California
Studied California College of Arts and
Crafts, Oakland, B.A. 1954
Mills College, Oakland, M.F.A. 1958
Teaches University of California, Davis
Resides Benicia

Robert Arneson is best known as a ceramic
sculptor. His first one-man exhibition was
at the Oakland Art Museum in 1960, and
he showed his work frequently in California
during the 1960s. In 1967 his work was
included in the "Funk Art" exhibition at the
University Art Museum, Berkeley. Arneson
became recognized as a draftsman only in
the late 1970s, and his drawings were the
focus of an exhibition at the Crocker Art
Museum, Sacramento, California, in 1983–
84. A major retrospective exhibition of his
work, which traveled throughout the United
States, was organized by the Des Moines
Art Center in 1986.

Reference Neal Benezra. *Robert Arneson:
A Retrospective*. Des Moines, 1985.

Rats
1981
Conté crayon, conté crayon wash, oil pastel,
and acrylic on wove paper
33 x 44¾" (83.5 x 113.5 cm)
1982-111-1

3 ALICE AYCOCK

Born 1946, Harrisburg, Pennsylvania
Studied Douglass College, New Brunswick,
New Jersey, B.A. 1968
Hunter College, New York, M.A. 1971
Teaches Hunter College, New York
Resides New York

Alice Aycock is noted for her sophisticated,
machinelike sculptures. Her early works
from the 1970s were large site-specific
pieces, and by the late 1970s and early
1980s, her fantasy constructions were being
shown in solo presentations, among them
*The Angels Continue Turning the Wheels of
the Universe Despite Their Ugly Souls . . .*
(1978) at the Salvatore Ala Gallery in Milan
and *The Large Scale Dis/Integration of
Micro-Electronic Memories* (1982) at the
Battery Park City Landfill in New York. In
1983–84, a retrospective of her projects and
ideas was organized by the Württembergischer Kunstverein in Stuttgart and traveled
extensively. In 1986, the La Jolla Museum
of Contemporary Art, California, included
her drawings in a group exhibition entitled
"Sitings," which also included Richard
Fleischner, Mary Miss, and George Trakas.
Her work has been shown in Italy, Japan,
and The Netherlands as part of the International Contemporary Sculpture Symposium
at Lake Biwa, Japan.

Reference Württembergischer Kunstverein,
Stuttgart. *Alice Aycock: Retrospective of
Projects and Ideas, 1972–1983*. 1983.

The Great God Pan
1980
Graphite on Mylar
42 x 51¾" (106.5 x 132 cm)
1981-36-1

4 JOHN BALDESSARI

Born 1931, National City, California
Studied San Diego State University, B.A.
1953; M.A. 1957
Teaches California Institute of Art, Los
Angeles
Resides Santa Monica, California

John Baldessari has become a well-known
Conceptual artist. His first exhibition was in
1960 at the La Jolla Museum of Contemporary Art, California, and by 1975 he had
received international recognition with a
one-man exhibition at the Stedelijk Museum
in Amsterdam. A major retrospective was
organized by The New Museum, New York,
and traveled in the United States in 1981–
82. More recent exhibitions in which Baldessari has participated include "Stills: Cinema
and Video Transformed" (1986) at the Seattle Art Museum and "This Is Not a Photograph: 20 Years of Large-Scale Photography,
1966–1986" (1987) at the John and Mable
Ringling Museum of Art, Sarasota, Florida.

Reference Marcia Tucker, Robert Pincus-
Witten, and Nancy Drew. *John Baldessari*.
New York, 1981.

Black Dice
1982
Nine color etchings in drypoint, aquatint,
sugar lift, soft ground, and photoetching on
Velin d'Arches paper, and photograph; edition 35 and 10 proofs; printed by Peter
Kneubühler, Zürich; published by Peter
Blum Edition, New York
6½ x 8" (16.3 x 20.5 cm) plates
1983-27-1a–i

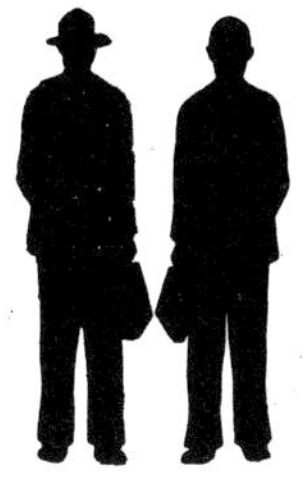 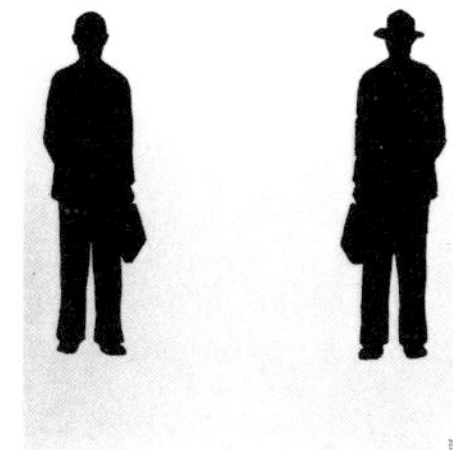 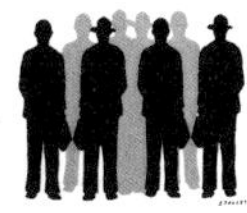 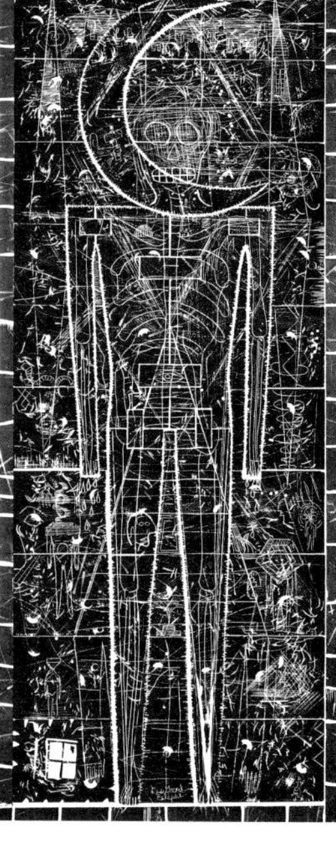

8

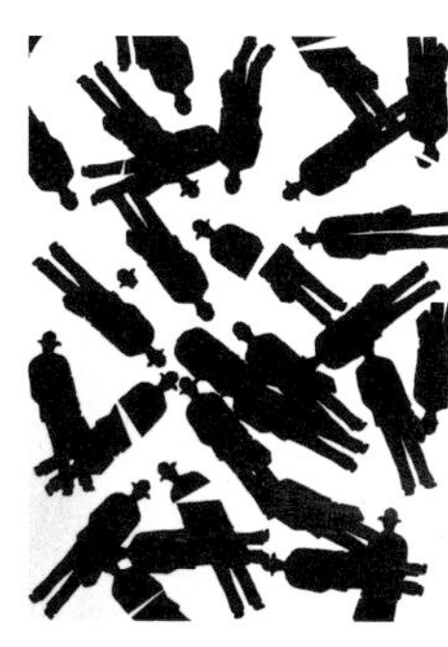

5 JENNIFER BARTLETT

Born 1941, Long Beach, California
Studied Mills College, Oakland, B.A. 1963
School of Art and Architecture, Yale University, New Haven, B.F.A. 1964; M.F.A. 1965
Resides New York

Jennifer Bartlett is known primarily for her multipartite paintings and prints. She has exhibited extensively in solo exhibitions since her first show at Mills College in 1963, notably in a recent traveling exhibition originating at the Walker Art Center, Minneapolis, in 1985. She has been included in group shows at The Museum of Modern Art, New York, since 1971; in three Whitney Biennial exhibitions (1977, 1979, 1981), "New Image Painting" (1978), and "Three Printmakers: Jennifer Bartlett, Susan Rothenberg, Terry Winters" (1986) at the Whitney Museum of American Art, New York; and in "Documenta" (1972, 1977) in Kassel, West Germany. Her prints have received attention in the National Print Exhibition (1983) at The Brooklyn Museum; in "Prints from Blocks: Gauguin to Now" (1983) at The Museum of Modern Art, New York; and in "70s into 80s: Printmaking Now" (1986–87) at the Museum of Fine Arts, Boston.

Reference Marge Goldwater, Roberta Smith, and Calvin Tomkins. *Jennifer Bartlett.* New York, 1985.

At Sea, Japan
1980
Six-part color woodcut with screenprint on Japanese handmade Kurotani Hosho paper; edition 58; Simca Print Artists, Tokyo
22½ x 99⅛" (57.6 x 251.8 cm) assembled
1981-14-1a–f

6 LORENZO BONECHI

Born 1955, Figline Valdarno, Italy
Studied Accademia di Belle Arti e Liceo Artistico, Florence
Resides Figline Valdarno

Lorenzo Bonechi's work was first shown in Rome in "La pittura colta" (1983), an exhibition at the Galleria Monti, and the following year he participated in "Metaphor and/or Symbol: A Perspective on Contemporary Art" (1984) at the National Museum of Modern Art, Tokyo. Bonechi first exhibited in the United States in 1985, in a one-man exhibition at the Sharpe Gallery, New York. His work was also included in "A New Romanticism: Sixteen Artists from Italy" at the Hirshhorn Museum and Sculpture Garden, Smithsonian Institution, Washington, D.C. (1985–86).

Reference Galleria Carini, Florence. *Lorenzo Bonechi.* 1985.

Saint Galganus
1985
Chalks on wove paper
47 x 59½" (120 x 150.4 cm)
1986-49-1

7 JONATHAN BOROFSKY

Born 1942, Boston
Studied Carnegie Mellon University, Pittsburgh, B.F.A. 1964
Ecole de Fontainebleau, France, 1964
School of Art and Architecture, Yale University, New Haven, M.F.A. 1966
Resides Venice, California

Jonathan Borofsky is known for his installations and, more recently, for his prints. His first one-man gallery exhibition was in New York in 1975, and the Wadsworth Atheneum in Hartford gave him his first museum show the following year. Borofsky has been represented in such major international exhibitions as the Whitney Biennial (1979, 1983) at the Whitney Museum of American Art, New York, and "Documenta" (1982) in Kassel, West Germany. His prints were included in the National Print Exhibition (1984) at The Brooklyn Museum, and his first major retrospective, which originated at the Philadelphia Museum of Art, traveled throughout the United States between 1984 and 1986.

Reference Mark Rosenthal and Richard Marshall. *Jonathan Borofsky.* Philadelphia, 1984.

2740475
1982
Portfolio of six drypoint etchings and seven silkscreens on Velin d'Arches paper; edition 50 and 10 artist's proofs; etchings printed by Robert Aull and Leslie Sutcliffe, Los Angeles; silkscreens printed by H. M. Büchi, Basel; published by Peter Blum Edition, New York
30 x 22" (76.2 x 55.9 cm) sheets
1983-28-1–13

8 JOHN BUCK

Born 1946, Ames, Iowa
Studied Kansas City Art Institute and School of Design, B.F.A. 1968
Skowhegan School of Sculpture and Painting, Maine, 1971
University of California, Davis, M.F.A. 1972
Teaches Montana State University, Bozeman
Resides Bozeman

John Buck's humorously metaphorical figural paintings and sculptures were exhibited in the Western states in the late 1970s and early 1980s. Recently he received national recognition for his woodcuts, which were exhibited in the National Print Exhibition (1984, 1986) at The Brooklyn Museum. He was also represented in "Awards in the Visual Arts 4" (1985) at the Albright-Knox Art Gallery, Buffalo.

Reference Yellowstone Art Center, Billings, Montana. *John Buck.* August 11–September 25, 1983.

Untitled
1983
Color woodcut on Suzu paper; edition 20 and 6 artist's proofs
75 x 31½" (190.5 x 80 cm) composition
1983-165-1

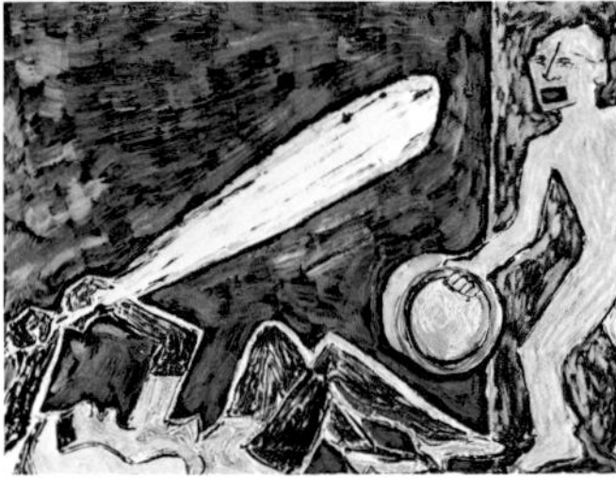

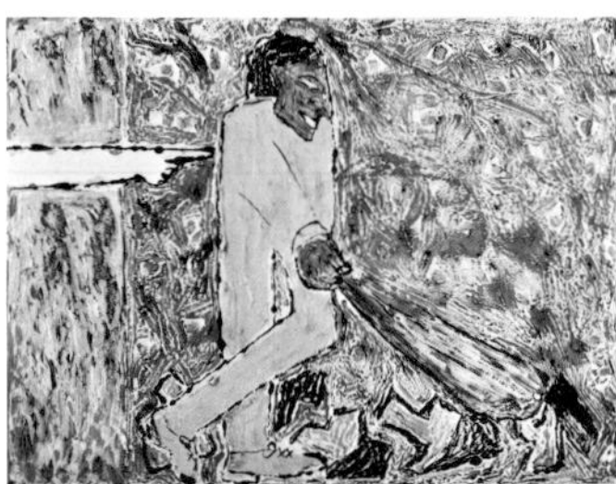

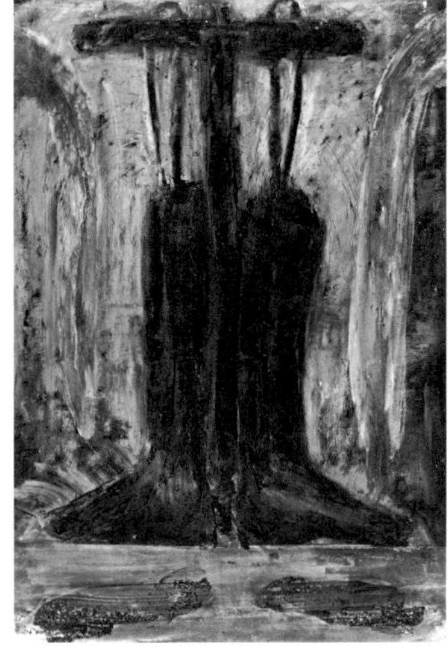

9 SUSAN BUSH

Born 1946, Wethersfield, Connecticut
Studied Mount Holyoke College, South Hadley, Massachusetts, B.A. 1968 Rosary College, River Forest, Illinois, at Villa Schifanoia, Florence, M.A. 1970; M.F.A. 1971
Resides New York

Susan Bush's first exhibition was in Seattle in 1965. Since then she has shown her work regularly, particularly in New England museums and galleries. In 1977 a solo exhibition, "Encaustics," was held at the Mejiro Gallery in Tokyo, and in 1984 she won an award in the 60th Annual International Competition at The Print Club, Philadelphia.

Woman with a Bat, no. 3 from the "Sleepless Nights" series
1981
Oil monotype with acrylic on wove paper
22¼ x 30″ (56.5 x 76.3 cm)
1982-6-1

Man with a Bat, no. 6 from the "Sleepless Nights" series
1981
Oil monotype with acrylic on wove paper
22¼ x 30″ (56.5 x 76.3 cm)
1982-6-2

10 BRUNO CECCOBELLI

Born 1952, Montecastello, Italy
Resides Rome

Bruno Ceccobelli exhibited his figurative work extensively in European galleries in the late 1970s and early 1980s. His work was shown in the exhibition "Bianchi, Ceccobelli, Dessì, Gallo" (1982) at the Groninger Museum, Groningen, The Netherlands. In the following year, Ceccobelli's work was introduced in the United States. Since then, he has had regular one-man and group gallery exhibitions at the Sperone Westwater Gallery in New York, as well as in Italy, France, West Germany, and The Netherlands.

Reference Sperone Westwater Gallery, New York. *De Umbris Idearum*. 1984.

Eudoia
1985
Oil and wax on paper
30½ x 22″ (77.5 x 55.7 cm)
1986-50-1

11 FRANCESCO CLEMENTE

Born 1952, Naples
Studied University of Rome
Resides Rome; Madras, India; and New York

Francesco Clemente is a self-taught painter who has a facility for working in a variety of mediums and uses remarkable coloring and imagery in his work. His first one-man exhibition was in Rome in 1971; he began showing regularly there with Gian Enzo Sperone in 1976 and by 1979 was exhibiting in Switzerland, The Netherlands, West Germany, and England. His first one-man show in the United States was held at the Sperone Westwater Fischer Gallery, New York, in 1980. More recent exhibitions of his work in the United States include "Francesco Clemente: Prints, 1981–1985" (1985) at the Metropolitan Museum of Art, New York, and "Francesco Clemente: The Departure of the Argonaut" (1986) at The Museum of Modern Art, New York. A retrospective, organized by the John and Mable Ringling Museum, Sarasota, Florida, traveled in the United States between 1985 and 1987.

Reference Michael Auping. *Francesco Clemente*. New York, 1985.

Italy
1983
Pastel on Rives wove paper
25¾ x 19″ (66 x 48.3 cm)
1984-8-1

12 ENZO CUCCHI

Born 1950, Morra d'Alba, Italy
Studied Accademia di Belle Arti, Macerata, Italy
Resides Ancona, Italy

Enzo Cucchi caught the public's attention in 1977 with a one-man show in Rome called "Ritratto di casa." He then exhibited at the São Paulo Bienal (1979) in Brazil; the Biennale des Jeunes (1980) in Paris; and the Venice Biennale (1980). He has been represented recently in "A New Romanticism: Sixteen Artists from Italy" (1985–86) at the Hirshhorn Museum and Sculpture Garden, Smithsonian Institution, Washington, D.C., and "Focus on the Image: Selections from the Rivendell Collection" (1986–90), which originated at the Phoenix Art Museum and is traveling throughout the United States. A one-man exhibition of his work was held at the Solomon R. Guggenheim Museum, New York, in 1986.

Reference Diane Waldman. *Enzo Cucchi*. New York, 1986.

A Dark Image
1982
Colored etching and aquatint on Fabriano Rosaspina paper; Arabic edition 30, Roman edition 6; printed by Valter Rossi at Vigna Antoniniana Stamperia d'Arte, Rome; published by Peter Blum Edition, New York
34½ x 54¼″ (87.4 x 137 cm) plate
1983-29-1

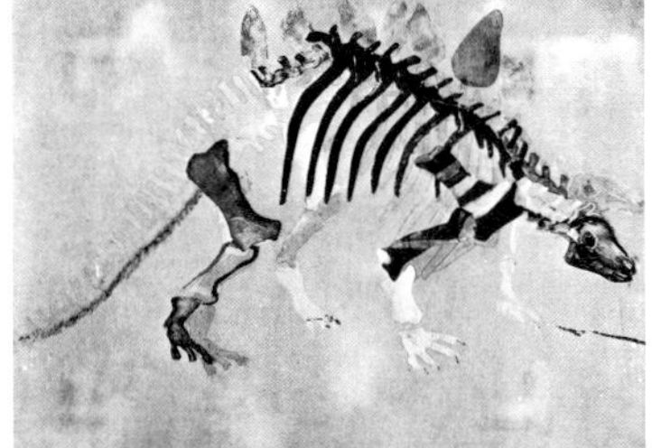

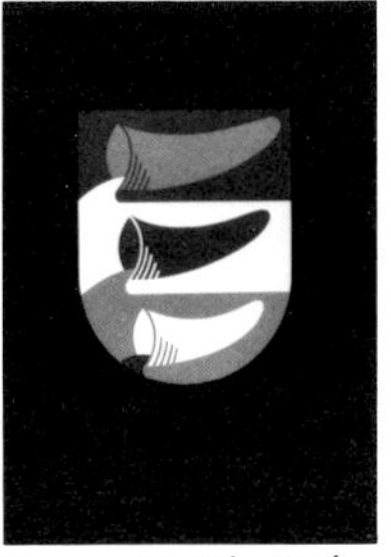

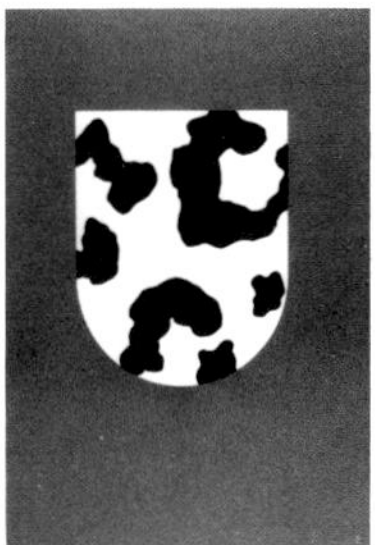

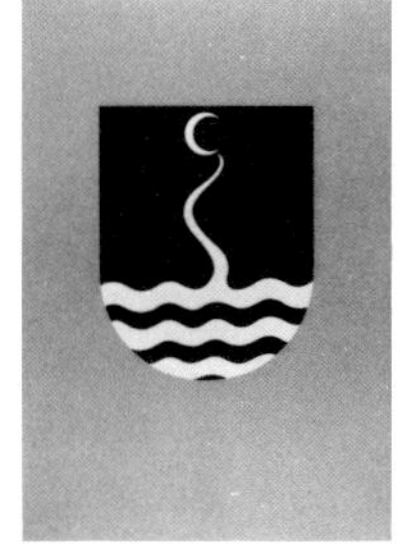

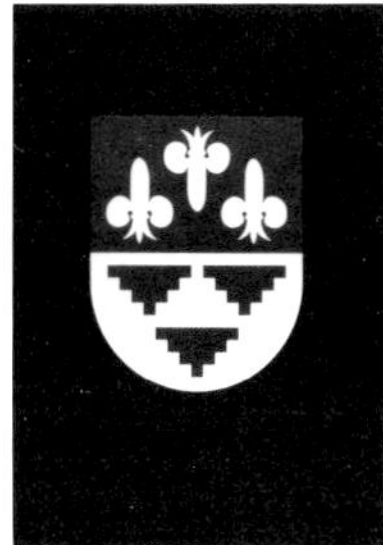

Cornucopia (The Birth of the Red, White, and Blue)

Dr. Blue Shield

The Honeymoon Is Over

Passion Over Reason

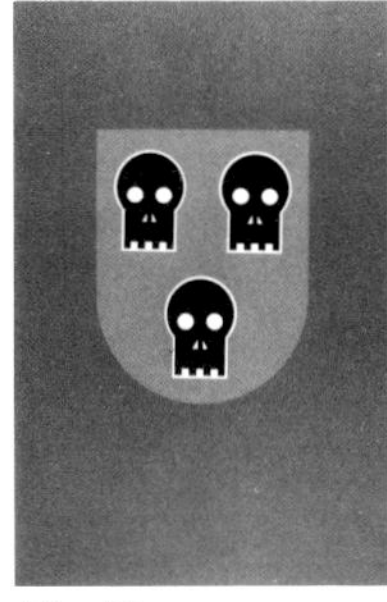

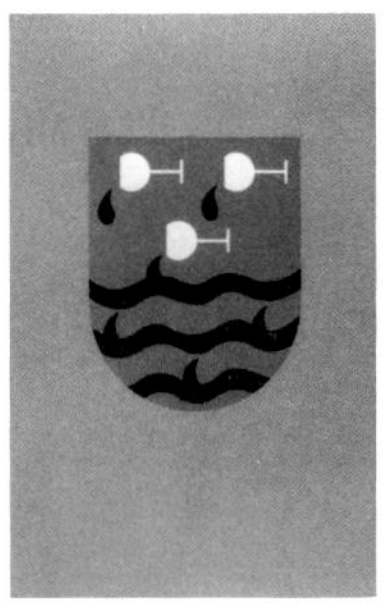

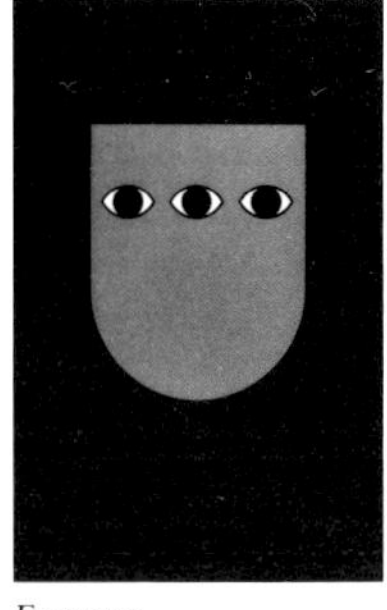

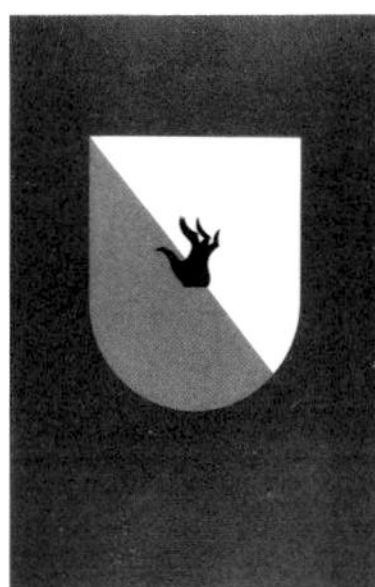

Nine Lives

Down the Drink

Eyeyeye

The Hand of the Spirit of Miss General Idea

---

13 JAN DIBBETS

Born 1941, Weert, The Netherlands
Studied Academie voor Beeldende en Bouwende Kunsten, Tilburg, The Netherlands, 1959–63
Saint Martin's School of Art, London, 1967
Resides Amsterdam

Jan Dibbets, whose work involves intricate photocollages, had his first exhibitions in the late 1960s in Europe. He has participated in major European group shows, including the Venice Biennale (1972) and "Documenta" (1972, 1982) in Kassel, West Germany. In the United States, Dibbets's work has been included in such group exhibitions as "Castelli and His Artists: Twenty-Five Years" (1982–83), which was organized by the Aspen Center for the Visual Arts, Colorado, and traveled extensively, and "The Real Big Picture" (1985–86) at The Queens Museum, New York. A retrospective exhibition was organized by the Walker Art Center, Minneapolis, in 1987, and was shown in New York, Detroit, West Palm Beach, and Eindhoven, The Netherlands.

Reference Martin Friedman, R. H. Fuchs, and M. M. M. Vos. *Jan Dibbets*. Minneapolis, 1987.

Untitled I, II, and III
1980
Three color lithographs with photocollage on board; edition 30; printed by Rento Brattingo, Amsterdam
28¾ x 28¾" (73 x 73 cm) sheets
1982-37-1a–c

---

14 ERIC FISCHL

Born 1948, New York
Studied California Institute of the Arts, Valencia, B.F.A. 1972
Resides New York

Eric Fischl's first one-man shows were in Canadian galleries in 1975 and 1976. Since the early 1980s his work has been seen in such group exhibitions as the Whitney Biennial (1983, 1985), the Venice Biennale (1984), and "Documenta" (1987) in Kassel, West Germany. The exhibition "Eric Fischl Paintings," which originated in 1985 at the Mendel Art Gallery, Saskatoon, Saskatchewan, Canada, traveled to Eindhoven, Basel, London, Toronto, Chicago, and New York. The evolution of two of his major print series, "Year of the Drowned Dog" and "Floating Islands," was examined in "Eric Fischl: Scenes Before the Eye," a traveling exhibition organized by the University Art Museum, California State University, Long Beach, in 1986.

Reference Constance W. Glenn and Lucinda Barnes. *Eric Fischl: Scenes Before the Eye.* Long Beach, California, 1986.

Year of the Drowned Dog
1983
Portfolio of six color etchings in aquatint, soft ground, drypoint, and scraping on Zerkall paper; edition 35 and 10 artist's proofs; printed by Peter Kneubühler, Zürich; published by Peter Blum Edition, New York
24⅝ x 70½" (62.5 x 179 cm) assembled
1983-164-1a–f

---

15 MARY FRANK

Born 1933, London
Studied American Art School, New York
Resides New York

Since her first solo exhibition in 1958 at the Poindexter Gallery, New York, Mary Frank has shown her work regularly throughout the United States, and is known especially for her monoprints and clay sculptures. Her monoprints were shown in "The Painterly Print: Monotypes from the Seventeenth to the Twentieth Century" (1980) at the Metropolitan Museum of Art, New York, "Contemporary Monotype: Six Masters" (1985) at the de Saisset Museum of Santa Clara University, California, and "Contemporary American Monotypes" (1985) at the Chrysler Museum, Norfolk, Virginia. Her work was also included in the National Print Exhibition (1984, 1986) at The Brooklyn Museum, where she was given a solo exhibition in 1987.

Reference de Saisset Museum, Santa Clara University, California. *Contemporary Monotype: Six Masters*. September 28–December 15, 1985.

Untitled (Dinosaur)
1980
Color monotype
25 x 34⅞" (63.3 x 88.7 cm) sheet
1980-95-1

---

16 GENERAL IDEA

• AA Bronson (Michael Tims)
   Born 1946, Vancouver, Canada
   Studied University of Manitoba, Canada, 1964–67
   Resides Toronto
• Felix Partz (Ron Gabe)
   Born 1945, Winnepeg, Canada
   Studied University of Manitoba, Canada, 1963–67
   Resides Toronto
• Jorge Zontal (Jorge Saia)
   Born 1944, Parma, Italy
   Studied Dalhousie University, Halifax, Nova Scotia, B. Arch., 1968
   Resides Toronto

These three artists came together in 1968 to work collaboratively under the appellation General Idea. They had their first solo exhibition in Toronto in 1971 and had shown internationally by 1978. Their most famous work, *The 1984 Miss General Idea Pavilion*, was exhibited at the Kunsthalle, Basel (1984), the Stedelijk van Abbemuseum, Eindhoven (1985), and the Albright-Knox Art Gallery, Buffalo (1986).

Reference Stedelijk van Abbemuseum, Eindhoven. *General Idea, 1968–1984.* January 12–February 17, 1985.

Fear Management
1987
Eight silkscreens on Rives BFK paper, hand painted by Winston Roeth; Arabic edition 50, Roman edition 10; printed by Sheila Marbain, Maurel Studios, New York; published by Peter Blum Edition, New York
33 x 22" (83.8 x 55.9 cm) sheets
1987-80-1–8

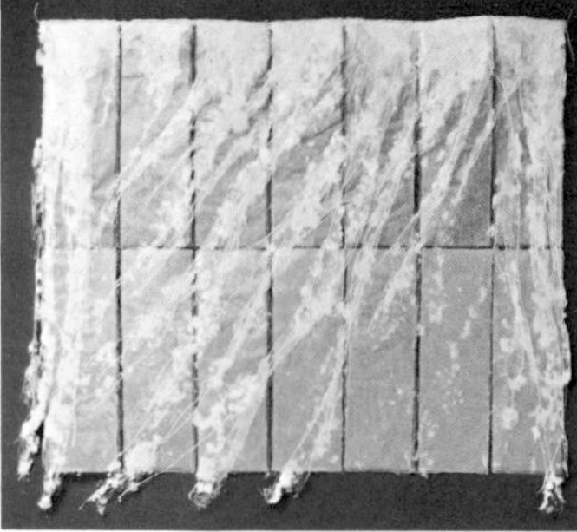

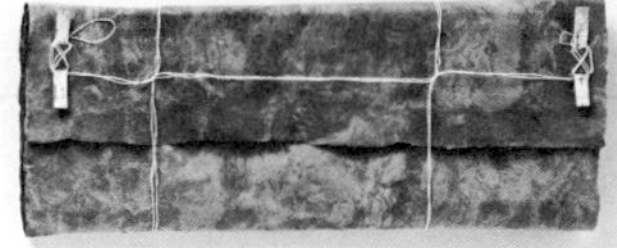

17 CAROLINE GREENWALD

Born 1936, Madison, Wisconsin
Studied University of Wisconsin, Madison,
B.S. 1957; M.A. 1975; M.F.A. 1977
Resides Madison, Wisconsin

Caroline Greenwald has been a frequent
exhibitor at group shows of handmade
paper and artist's books. Her first solo exhibition was in 1975 at the Humanities Gallery of the University of Wisconsin, and in
1977 she participated in "New Ways with
Paper" at the National Collection of Fine
Arts, Smithsonian Institution, Washington,
D.C. She has traveled extensively, studying
paper and establishing temporary studios in
Tokyo (1983–84) and Paris (1987). Recent
group exhibitions include "Paper Now:
Bent, Molded, and Manipulated" (1986–
87) at The Cleveland Museum of Art and
the "Concours Internationale du Livres
d'Artistes" (1986–87) in Montreal, Canada.

Reference Sakura Gallery, Nagoya, Japan.
The Tender Cry of Wind. 1985.

Snow Cloud Markings, from the "Map"
series
1978
Japanese handmade Tengujo paper, rag, and
abaca paper pulps, line, wool fibers, and
size in a dark amate map case with birch
bark clasps
6½ x 16¼ x 1⅜" (16.4 x 41.2 x 3.4 cm)
closed
31½ x 35½" (80 x 91 cm) open
1979-140-1

18 JÖRG IMMENDORFF

Born 1945, Bleckede, West Germany
Studied Kunstakademie, Düsseldorf,
1963–64
Resides Düsseldorf

Jörg Immendorff's first one-man exhibition
was held at the New Orleans Club in Bonn
in 1961. By the 1970s he had participated in
such international group exhibitions as
"Documenta" (1972) in Kassel, West Germany, and the Venice Biennale (1976). In
the 1980s Immendorff gained further international recognition through exhibitions at
galleries in Amsterdam, Bern, Madrid, Paris,
Ghent, Milan, and New York. His work was
included in "Expressions: New Art from
Germany" (1983–84) at the Saint Louis Art
Museum and "German Art in the Twentieth
Century" (1985) at the Royal Academy of
Arts in London. A major one-man exhibition of his work was held at the Kunstverein
Braunschweig, Brunswick, West Germany,
in 1985.

Reference Kunstverein Braunschweig,
Brunswick, West Germany. *Jörg Immendorff.* March 29–May 12, 1985.

Cities of Motion, Berlin, from the "Café
Deutschland gut" series
1983
Color linocut with hand coloring; printed
by the artist and assistants, Düsseldorf;
published by Maximilian Verlag and Sabine
Knust, Munich
69¾ x 90¼" (177.2 x 229.3 cm) sheet
1985-40-1

19 YVONNE JACQUETTE

Born 1934, Pittsburgh
Studied Rhode Island School of Design,
Providence, 1956
Resides New York

Yvonne Jacquette's first solo exhibitions of
her aerial cityscapes were held in the Philadelphia area—at Swarthmore College
(1965) and at the Tyler School of Art, Temple University (1972). Although she has
exhibited primarily on the East Coast, Jacquette has also had shows in St. Louis, San
Francisco, and Tokyo. Her prints have become increasingly appreciated, and were
included in the National Print Exhibition
(1984, 1986) at The Brooklyn Museum, in
"Monotypes" (1983) at the State University
of New York at Purchase, and in "Interiors
and Exteriors: Contemporary Realist
Prints" (1986) at the Yale University Art
Gallery, New Haven.

Reference Bowdoin College Museum of
Art, Brunswick, Maine. *Yvonne Jacquette:
Tokyo Nightviews.* June 27–August 24,
1986.

Aerial View of 33rd Street
1981
Three-color lithograph on Transpagra;
edition 60, 11 artist's proofs, 3 printer's
proofs, and 1 *bon à tirer*; printed by Chris
Erickson and Rodrigo Shopis, New York;
published by Brooke Alexander Inc., New
York
50 x 31" (126.9 x 78.9 cm) sheet
1982-7-1

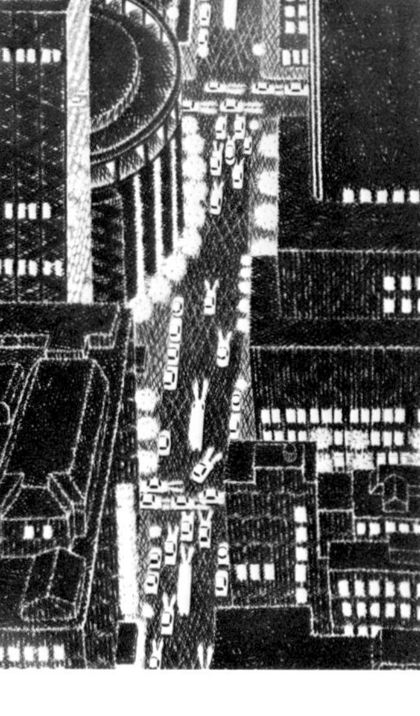

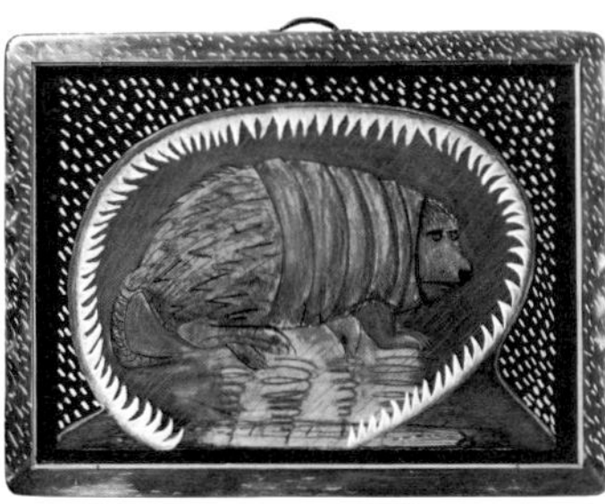

20 MAURIE KERRIGAN

Born 1951, Jersey City
Studied Moore College of Art, Philadelphia
B.F.A. 1973
The Art Institute of Chicago, M.F.A. 1977
Resides Philadelphia

Maurie Kerrigan's sensitively humorous
work had its first solo exhibition, "No Fish-
ing Today" (1976), at Etage in Philadelphia.
She has participated in numerous group
shows throughout the United States, including "Awards in the Visual Arts 1" (1982),
which was shown in Washington, D.C., Des
Moines, and Denver. Following two succes-
sive fellowships at the MacDowell Colony
in 1986 and 1987, Kerrigan had her first solo
museum exhibition at the Philadelphia Museum of Art.

Reference Maurie Kerrigan. *Rockin': Forty
Drawings.* Philadelphia, 1987.

Moth Eating a Whole in My New Sweater
1985
Charcoal, pastel, and oil pastel on paper
with artist-made frame
27¼ x 36½" (69.3 x 92.8 cm) framed
1985-41-1

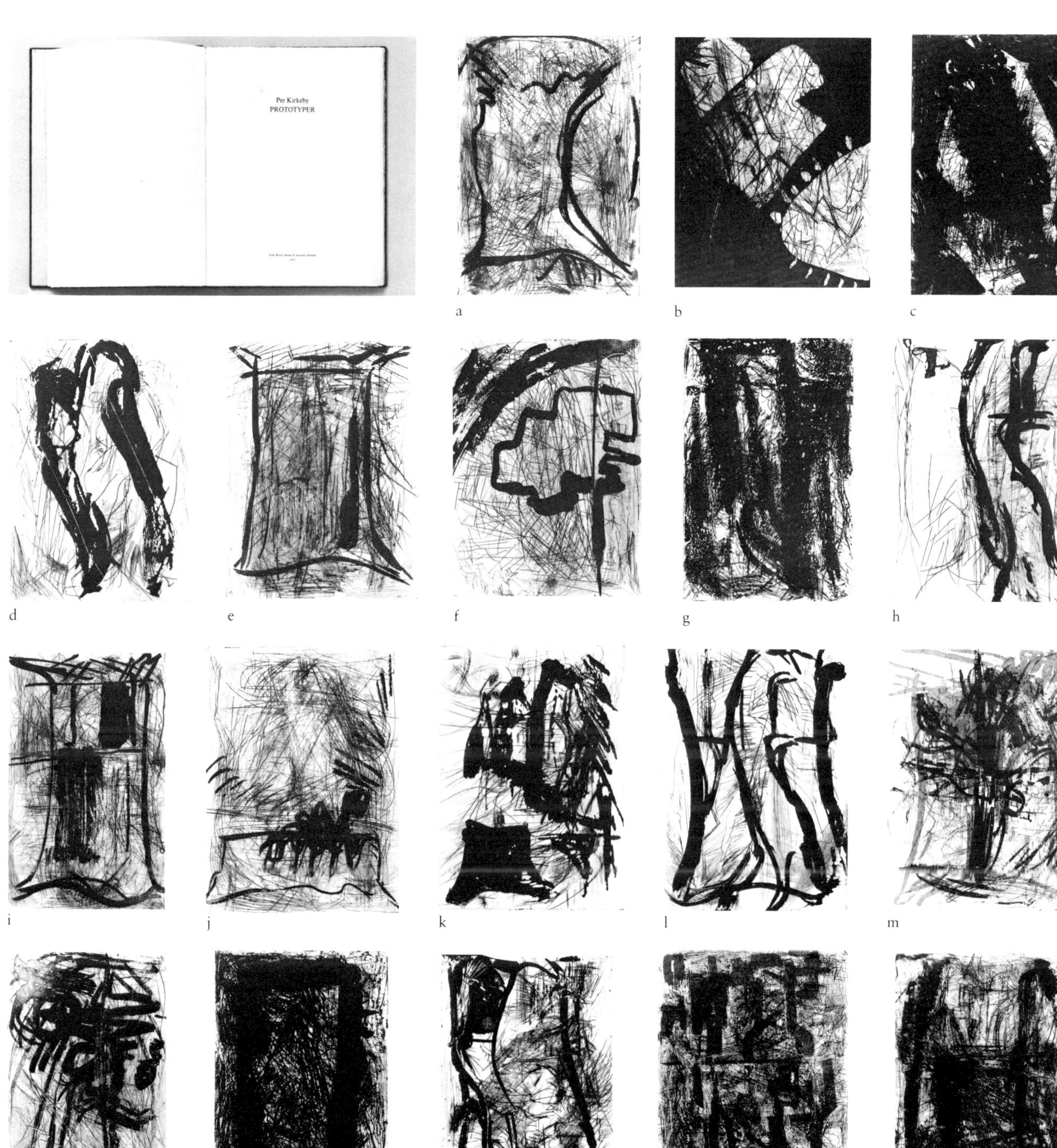

a
b
c
d
e
f
g
h
i
j
k
l
m
n
o
p
q
r

21 PER KIRKEBY

Born 1938, Copenhagen, Denmark
Studied University of Copenhagen, 1957–64
Experimental Art School, Copenhagen, 1962
Resides Copenhagen

Per Kirkeby began his career as a painter and sculptor in the early 1960s, after having received a doctorate in geology. His first solo exhibitions were in Copenhagen galleries, but by the mid 1970s he was known throughout Europe, and his work was included in the Venice Biennale of 1976. At that time he also became known for his prints and drawings. His work was introduced to the United States in 1982 in the exhibition "Art Now: Contemporary Scandinavian Art" at the Solomon R. Guggenheim Museum, New York. Since then he has shown in several gallery exhibitions in New York and in the 1985 Carnegie International at the Carnegie Institute in Pittsburgh.

Reference Kunstverein Braunschweig, Brunswick, West Germany. *Per Kirkeby.* 1984.

Prototypes
1983
Book of eighteen plates of various sizes: etching, aquatint, and drypoint on Arches paper; edition 19; printed by Niels Borch Jensen, Copenhagen; published by Niels Borch Jensen and Susanne Ottesen, Copenhagen
15⅛ x 11⅛″ (38.3 x 28.2 cm) sheets
1986-51-1a–r

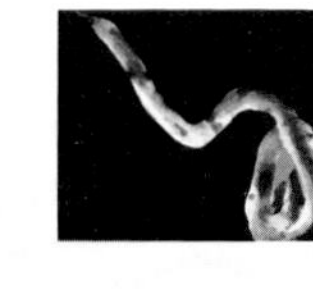
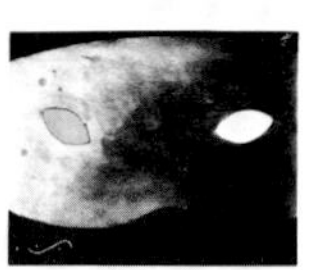
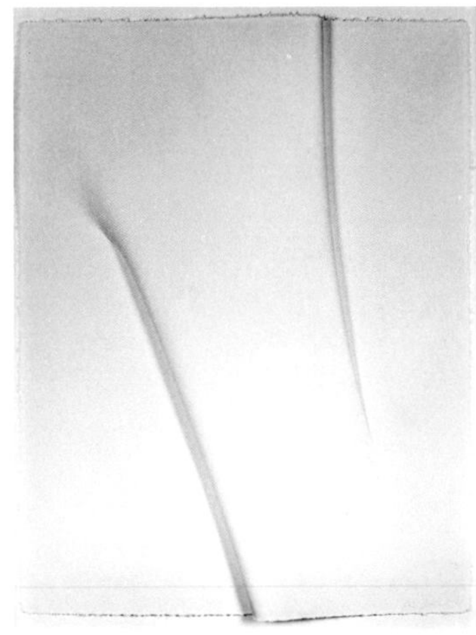

22 BARBARA KRUGER

Born 1945, Newark, New Jersey
Studied Syracuse University, New York, 1965
Parsons School of Design, New York, 1966
Resides New York

Barbara Kruger's work was exhibited in 1973 at the Whitney Biennial at the Whitney Museum of American Art, New York, and in 1974 she had her first solo exhibition at Artists Space, New York. However, it was not until 1982 that her work, which combines words and photographic images, attracted international attention at "Documenta" in Kassel, West Germany, and at the Venice Biennale. Solo exhibitions have recently been organized by the Los Angeles County Museum of Art (1985), the Wadsworth Atheneum in Hartford (1985), the Contemporary Arts Museum, Houston, Texas (1985), and the Krannert Art Museum of the University of Illinois (1986).

Reference Mary Boone Gallery, New York. *Barbara Kruger.* 1987.

Untitled
1985
Nine color lithographs with photo plates, hand-drawn plates, and silkscreen on Arches 88 paper; Arabic edition 50, Roman edition 10; printed by Maurice Sanchez and assistants at Derrière l'Etoile Studios, New York; published by Peter Blum Edition, New York
20½ x 20½" (52 x 52 cm) sheets
1986-131-1–9

23 ROBERT KUSHNER

Born 1949, Pasadena, California
Studied University of California, San Diego, B.A. 1971
Resides New York

Robert Kushner's exhibition and performance "Costumes for Moving Bodies" (1971) at the Art Gallery of the University of California, San Diego, indicated an interest in fabric and pattern that was to be a constant in his work. Between 1975 and 1985, he was included in such group exhibitions as the Whitney Biennial (1975, 1981, 1985) at the Whitney Museum of American Art, New York, the Venice Biennale (1980, 1984), and the National Print Exhibition (1984, 1986) at The Brooklyn Museum. The Institute of Contemporary Art of the University of Pennsylvania held a mid-career summary of Kushner's work in 1987.

Reference Janet Kardon. *Robert Kushner.* Philadelphia, 1987.

Cupids Gardening
1981
Two-color, three-panel lithograph on Arches paper with Japanese Mingei paper *chine collé*; edition 20 and 6 artist's proofs; printed by Judith Solodkin at Solo Press, New York
90 x 23½" (228.6 x 59.6 cm) assembled
1981-91-1

24 LOIS LANE

Born 1948, Philadelphia
Studied Philadelphia College of Art, B.F.A. 1969
School of Art and Architecture, Yale University, New Haven, M.F.A. 1971
Resides New York

Lois Lane's oil paintings and collages first received public attention in the group exhibition "New Image Painting" (1978–79) at the Whitney Museum of American Art, New York, and a solo exhibition of paintings and collages was organized by the Akron Art Museum, Ohio, in 1980. Her prints have become increasingly well known in recent years, and she was represented at the National Print Exhibition (1984) at The Brooklyn Museum. Her prints were featured in a solo exhibition at the Willard Gallery, New York, in 1987.

Reference Richard Marshall. *New Image Painting.* New York, 1978.

Untitled
1981
Color aquatint, soft ground, spit bite, and gold leaf; edition 35 and 12 artist's proofs; printed by Aeropress, New York; published by Parasol Press Ltd., New York
15¾ x 19½" (40 x 49.5 cm) plate
1982-38-1

Untitled
1981
Color aquatint, soft ground, spit bite, and gold leaf; edition 35 and 12 artist's proofs; printed by Aeropress, New York; published by Parasol Press Ltd., New York
15¾ x 19½" (40 x 49.5 cm) plate
1982-38-2

25 LOUIS LIEBERMAN

Born 1944, Brooklyn
Studied Brooklyn College, B.A. 1965
Brooklyn Museum Art School, 1964
Rhode Island School of Design, Providence, B.F.A. 1969
Resides New York

Louis Lieberman's distinctive handmade paper works have been included in numerous group exhibitions in the 1970s and 1980s. Since his first one-man exhibition in 1969 in Vancouver he has regularly exhibited on the East Coast. He was represented in the exhibition "Art on Paper, 1986" at the Weatherspoon Art Gallery of the University of North Carolina, Greensboro, and in "Art Cake, 1980–1987" at the Kunsthaus in Zürich.

#28
1979
Cast paper
34 x 26" (87 x 66 cm)
1980-20-1

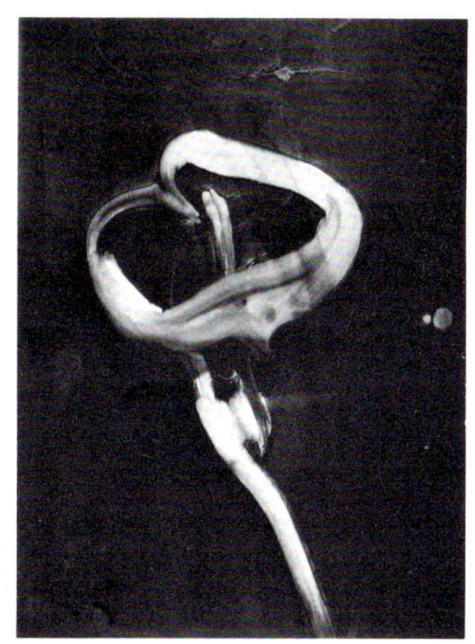

26 RICHARD LONG

Born 1945, Bristol, England
Studied West of England College of Art, Bristol, 1962–65
Saint Martin's School of Art, London, 1966–68
Resides Bristol

Richard Long's work has been shown in Europe and the United States every year since 1968. His stone works, maps, and word pieces have been included in such major group exhibitions as "Documenta" (1972, 1982) in Kassel, West Germany, and the Venice Biennale (1980). In the mid 1980s, Long began to make mud drawings directly on walls and on paper, and this new direction was also represented in his solo exhibition at the Solomon R. Guggenheim Museum, New York, in 1986.

Reference R. H. Fuchs. *Richard Long.* New York, 1986.

Mud Foot Circles
1985
Mud on paper laid on board
76⅜ x 87½" (194 x 222 cm)
1987-14-1

27 NINO LONGOBARDI

Born 1953, Naples, Italy
Resides Naples

Nino Longobardi's distinctive figural imagery first came to public attention in gallery exhibitions in Cologne and Naples in 1978. The exhibition "Italian Art Now: An American Perspective" (1982) at the Solomon R. Guggenheim Museum, New York, introduced his work into the United States. In the same year, Longobardi participated in the group exhibition "Avanguardia e Transavanguardia" at the Galleria Mura Aureliane in Rome. In 1984 he had a solo exhibition at the Metropolitan Museum of Art, New York, and was included in "An International Survey of Recent Paintings and Sculpture" at The Museum of Modern Art, New York. He was represented in "Representation Abroad: Diversity" (1985) at the Hirshhorn Museum and Sculpture Garden, Smithsonian Institution, Washington, D.C., and in the Paris Biennale (1985).

Reference Galerie Bugdahn & Szeimes, Düsseldorf. *Nino Longobardi.* March 6–April 30, 1987.

Untitled
1983
Gesso, charcoal, and wash on three pieces of paper
30½ x 66" (77.5 x 167.7 cm) assembled
1984-74-1

28 MICHAEL MAZUR

Born 1935, New York
Studied Accademia di Belle Arti e Liceo Artistico, Florence, 1956–57
Amherst College, Massachusetts, B.A. 1958
School of Art and Architecture, Yale University, New Haven, B.F.A. 1959; M.F.A. 1961
Resides Cambridge, Massachusetts

Michael Mazur is well known for his graphic work, particularly his monotypes. One of his first exhibitions was a one-man show at The Print Club, Philadelphia, in 1964. He has consistently exhibited since the 1960s, participating in the National Print Exhibition (1964, 1966, 1976, 1983, 1986) at The Brooklyn Museum, "The Painterly Print: Monotypes from the Seventeenth to the Twentieth Century" (1980) at the Metropolitan Museum of Art, New York, and "American Realism: Twentieth-Century Drawings and Watercolors" (1985), which traveled extensively, originating at the San Francisco Museum of Modern Art. A one-man exhibition of Mazur's work was held at Beaver College, Glenside, Pennsylvania, in 1986.

Reference Michael Mazur. *Self-Portraits.* New York, 1986.

Gesture of a Calla, xii
1985
Monotype on wove paper
29¾ x 22¼" (75.6 x 56.5 cm) sheet
1987-38-1

29 ELIZABETH MURRAY

Born 1940, Chicago
Studied The Art Institute of Chicago, B.F.A. 1962
Mills College, Oakland, M.F.A. 1964
Resides New York

Since her first solo exhibition in 1975 at a gallery in Toronto, Murray has shown annually in galleries and museums across the United States. The first museum survey of her work, organized by the Dallas Museum of Art and the Massachusetts Institute of Technology in 1987–88, is traveling extensively in the United States. Murray's drawings have recently been featured in exhibitions at the Carnegie Mellon University Art Gallery, Pittsburgh (1986), and at the University Art Museum of the University of California, Berkeley (1987). Her prints were included in the National Print Exhibition (1986) at The Brooklyn Museum.

Reference Sue Graze, Kathy Halbreich, and Roberta Smith. *Elizabeth Murray: Paintings and Drawings.* New York, 1987.

Second Painter's Partner
1980
Pastel on three pieces of Fabriano CMF wove paper
29 x 85⅜" (73.6 x 216.9 cm) assembled
1981-17-1

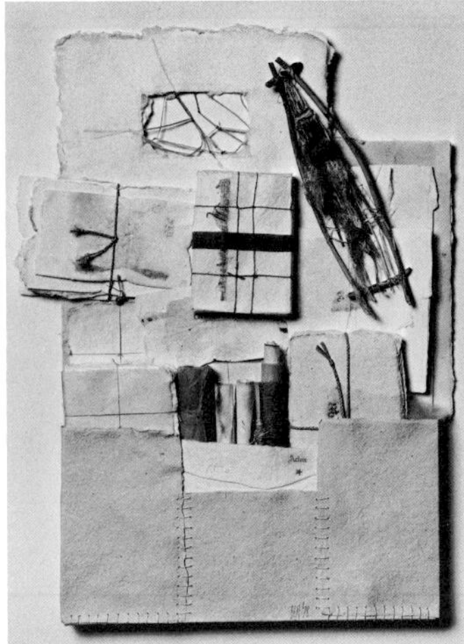

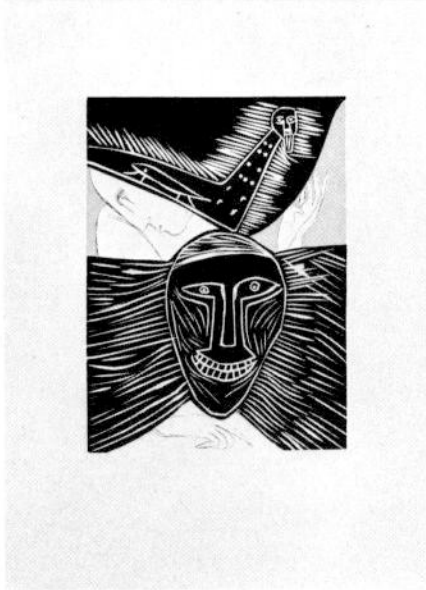

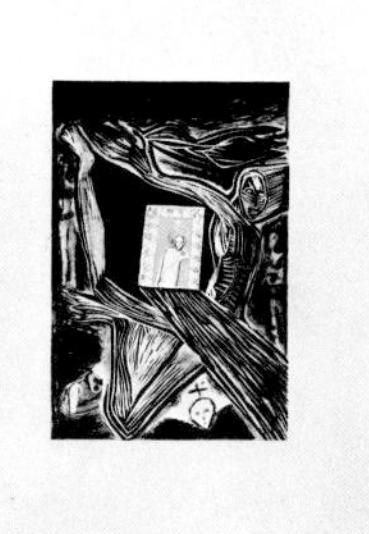

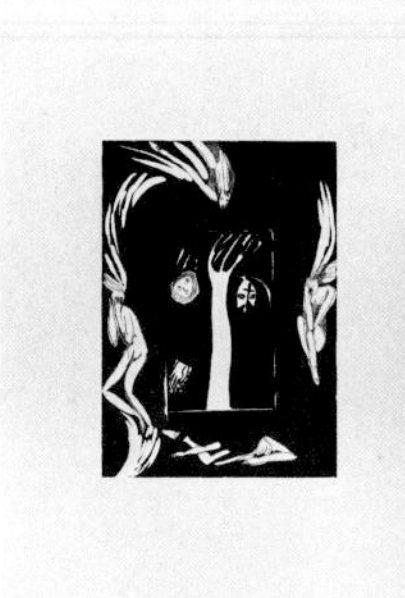

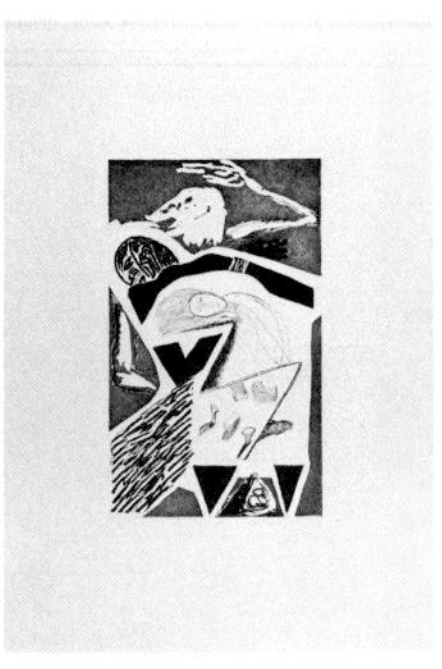

I   2   3   4

30 ROBERT NUGENT

Born 1947, Santa Monica, California
Studied College of Creative Studies, University of California, Santa Barbara, B.F.A. 1969
University of California, Santa Barbara, M.F.A. 1971
Teaches Sonoma State University, Rohnert Park, California
Resides Rohnert Park

Robert Nugent, known for his intricate and mystical paper works, first exhibited at the Art Galleries of the University of California, Santa Barbara, in a group show in 1968 and in a one-man show in 1971. He has shown every year since then, primarily in California. He has traveled twice to Brazil, once in 1984 on a travel grant from the California State University, and again in 1986 on a Fulbright Foundation Grant for Travel, and has had an exhibition at the Museu de Arte in São Paulo. Since that time his work has profoundly changed and he now works mostly in pastel.

Reference Museu de Arte de São Paulo, Brazil. *Bob L. Nugent: Série dos Jardins.* June 5–22, 1986.

The Acteon, from "The Ancient Mariner" series
1978
Handmade papers, wood, straw, string, beads, bark, and wool
16¾ x 12⅝" (42.4 x 32.2 cm) composition
1979-141-1

31 DENNIS OPPENHEIM

Born 1938, Electric City, Washington
Studied California College of Arts and Crafts, Oakland, B.F.A. 1965
Stanford University, Palo Alto, California, M.F.A. 1965
Resides New York

Dennis Oppenheim, now well known for his fantasy constructions, was strongly under the influence of California funk art in the early 1960s. In 1968 he participated in the group exhibition "Earthworks" at the Dwan Gallery, New York. In the 1970s he became more concerned with installations and large-scale constructions, and in 1981 he participated in the exhibition "Machineworks" at the Institute of Contemporary Art, University of Pennsylvania, Philadelphia. A survey of his work was shown at the Eric Franck Gallery in Geneva in 1984.

Reference Eric Franck Gallery, Geneva. *Dennis Oppenheim.* 1984.

. . . And the Mind Grew Fingers
1984
Graphite, crayon, ink, charcoal, oil wash, and oil pastel on wove paper
50⅛ x 38¼" (127.3 x 97.2 cm)
1984-46-1

32 MIMMO PALADINO

Born 1948, Paduli, Italy
Studied Liceo Artistico di Benevento, Italy, 1964–68
Resides Paduli and Milan

Mimmo Paladino's first solo exhibitions took place in the late 1970s at galleries in northern Italy. As part of the group of Italian artists called the Transavanguardia, he has been included in such major group exhibitions as the Venice Biennale (1980), "Documenta" (1982) in Kassel, West Germany, and "Recent European Painting" (1983) at the Solomon R. Guggenheim Museum, New York. By the mid 1980s, having achieved international recognition, Paladino's work was being represented in several major American group shows: "A New Romanticism: Sixteen Artists from Italy" (1985–86) at the Hirshhorn Museum and Sculpture Garden, Smithsonian Institution, Washington, D.C.; "New Art of Italy" at the Joslyn Art Museum, Omaha (1985–86); and "Focus on the Image: Selections from the Rivendell Collection" (1986–90) at the Phoenix Art Museum.

Reference Howard N. Fox. *A New Romanticism: Sixteen Artists from Italy.* Washington, D.C., 1985.

Between the Wind and the Fire
1982
Color etching with hard ground, spit bite, aquatint, drypoint, and linocut on Arches paper; edition 35 and 12 artist's proofs; printed by Aeropress, New York
15⅞ x 9½" (40.4 x 24.4 cm) plate
1982-74-1

Watching Mysteries
1982
Color etching with hard ground, aquatint, and linocut on Arches paper; edition 35 and 12 artist's proofs; printed by Aeropress, New York
15½ x 11¾" (39.1 x 29.8 cm) plate
1982-74-2

Stars on the Scene
1982
Color etching with hard ground, aquatint, and linocut on Arches paper; edition 35 and 12 artist's proofs; printed by Aeropress, New York
14⅞ x 10½" (37.6 x 26.8 cm) plate
1982-74-3

Menacing Caverns
1982
Color etching with hard ground, spit bite, aquatint, drypoint, and linocut on Arches paper; edition 35 and 12 artist's proofs; printed by Aeropress, New York
15⅞ x 9½" (40.4 x 24.4 cm) plate
1982-74-4

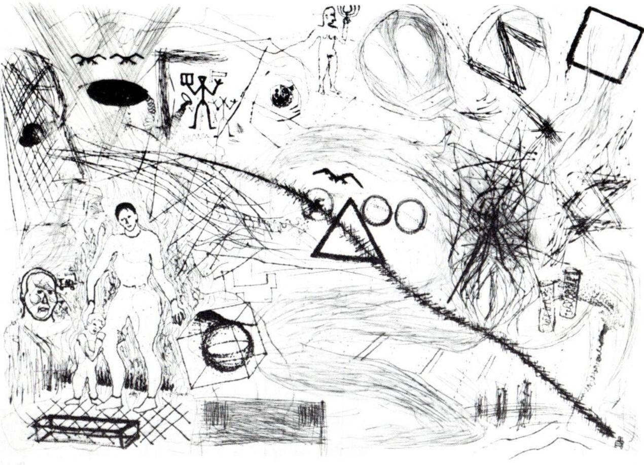

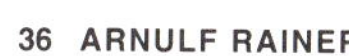

33 A. R. PENCK (Ralf Winkler)

Born 1939, Dresden
Resides London

A. R. Penck's first solo exhibition was at Galerie Michael Werner in Cologne in 1969. By the mid 1970s he was exhibiting his paintings, prints, drawings, and sculptures at such major international shows as "Documenta" (1972, 1982) at Kassel, West Germany, and the Venice Biennale (1976). In 1983 "Expressions: New Art from Germany," organized by the Saint Louis Art Museum, introduced Penck's work in the United States. A major one-man exhibition took place at Kunstverein Braunschweig, Brunswick, West Germany, in 1985–86.

Reference Kunstverein Braunschweig, Brunswick, West Germany. *A. R. Penck.* 1985–86.

Thoughts in a Kibbutz, from the portfolio *Expedition to the Holy Land*
1984
Drypoint, etching, and roulette work on Arches paper; Arabic edition 50, Hebrew letter edition 14, and 16 artist's proofs; printed by Burston Graphics Centre, Jerusalem; published by Joshua Gessel, Tel Aviv
25½ x 36¾" (64.8 x 93.3 cm) plate
1984-92-1

34 HOWARDENA PINDELL

Born 1943, Philadelphia
Studied Boston University, B.F.A. 1965 School of Art and Architecture, Yale University, New Haven, M.F.A. 1967
Teaches State University of New York, Stony Brook
Resides New York

Howardena Pindell has been exhibiting her elaborate paper works since 1969, when she was represented in the "American Drawing Biennial XXIII" at the Norfolk Museum of Arts and Sciences, Virginia. Her first solo show was in the Rockefeller Memorial Galleries, Spellman College, Atlanta, in 1971. She participated in several group exhibitions in 1986, including "Adornments" at the Bernice Steinbaum Gallery, New York, "Hidden Heritage" at the Bronx Museum, New York, and "Transitions: The Afro-American Artist" at the Bergen Museum of Art and Science, Paramus, New Jersey. A solo exhibition took place at the Studio Museum in Harlem, New York, in 1986.

Reference The Studio Museum in Harlem, New York. *Howardena Pindell: Odyssey.* February 12–June 12, 1986.

Untitled No. 89
1977
Acrylic, gouache, watercolor, thread, glitter, and cut paper on board
14⅜ x 10½" (36.5 x 26.7 cm)
1979-142-1

35 JODY PINTO

Born 1942, New York
Studied Pennsylvania Academy of the Fine Arts, Philadelphia, 1964–68 Philadelphia College of Art, B.F.A. 1973
Teaches Pennsylvania Academy of the Fine Arts
Resides New York

Jody Pinto first exhibited her large-scale site work in 1975 at Artpark in Lewiston, New York. Since that time, she has had numerous public commissions and is recognized for her masterful drawings and models. She has participated in the Whitney Biennial (1979) at the Whitney Museum of American Art, New York, and in the Venice Biennale (1980). Her most recent project in Philadelphia, the *Fingerspan* pedestrian bridge, was completed in Fairmount Park in 1987 and accompanied by an exhibition of related drawings at the Marian Locks Gallery. Pinto has also recently become involved in performance works and their accompanying sets and costumes; in 1986 she worked on the performance *Practical Spirits . . .* at Temple University Theater, Philadelphia.

Reference Institute of Contemporary Art, University of Pennsylvania, Philadelphia. *Jody Pinto: The Henri Drawings.* June 13–July 29, 1984.

Split Tongue Pier
1980
Crayon, graphite, and watercolor on wove paper
39⅛ x 59" (99.3 x 149.9 cm)
1981-19-1

36 ARNULF RAINER

Born 1929, Baden, Austria
Teaches Akademie der bildenden Künste, Vienna
Resides Vienna, Upper Austria, and Bavaria

Arnulf Rainer has explored many concepts, styles, and mediums, but is probably most recognized today for his images overworked with monochromatic coats of paint, and for his self-portraits, which are also partially erased and effaced surfaces. From 1953 to 1959 he showed several times at the influential Austrian Galerie St. Stephan. Since the 1950s Rainer has had numerous one-man exhibitions in Europe, notably at the Kunsthalle, Bern (1977), at the Nationalgalerie, Berlin (1981), and at the Centre Georges Pompidou, Paris (1984). In the United States he has exhibited at the Busch-Reisinger Museum, Cambridge, Massachusetts (1972), and at the Walker Art Center, Minneapolis (1980).

Reference Nationalgalerie (West Germany), Berlin. *Arnulf Rainer.* November 20, 1980–February 4, 1981.

Red Cross
1981–84
Color drypoint; edition 35, artist's proof; printed by Karl Imhof, Munich
45 x 19½" (114.2 x 48.5 cm) plate
1987-83-1

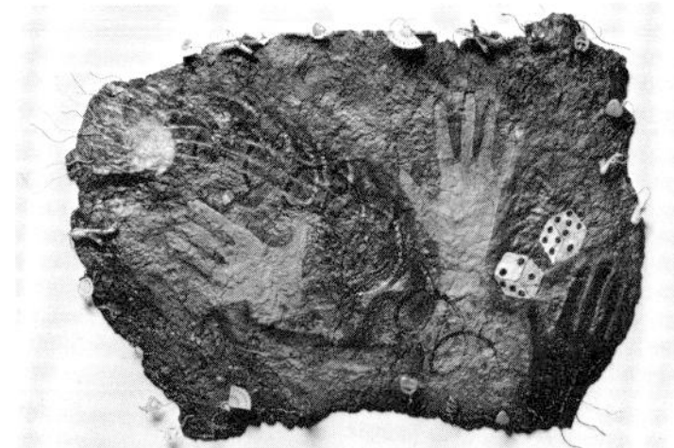

38

39

37 SUSAN ROTHENBERG

Born 1945, Buffalo, New York
Studied Cornell University, Ithaca, B.F.A. 1967
Resides New York

The first exhibitions of Susan Rothenberg's paintings and drawings took place primarily in New York in the mid 1970s. By 1980 her work had been shown at the Whitney Biennial (1979) at the Whitney Museum of American Art, New York, and at the Venice Biennale (1980). She had two solo exhibitions in the following two years, one at the Stedelijk Museum, Amsterdam (1982), and another organized by the Los Angeles County Museum of Art, which traveled from 1983 to 1985. Recently, Rothenberg's prints have also received attention, being included in "Issues in Contemporary Prints, 1974–1983" (1984) at the Fogg Art Museum, Cambridge, Massachusetts, "Three Printmakers: Jennifer Bartlett, Susan Rothenberg, Terry Winters" (1986) at the Whitney Museum of American Art, New York, and the National Print Exhibition (1984, 1986) at The Brooklyn Museum.

Reference Rachel Robertson Maxwell. *Susan Rothenberg: The Prints*. Philadelphia, 1987.

Untitled
1983
Drypoint, aquatint, burnishing, and etching on Somerset Satin paper; edition 35 and 9 proofs; printed (by Charles Levine) and published at Mountain Shadow Studio, Highland, New York
25½ x 21⅝" (63.5 x 54.9 cm) plate
1984-10-1

38 BETYE SAAR

Born 1926, Los Angeles
Studied University of California, Los Angeles, B.A. 1949
California State University, Long Beach, 1958–62
Resides Los Angeles

Betye Saar first exhibited her assemblages in the late 1960s in California. Her work was seen in "The Drawing Show" (1973) at Womanspace, Los Angeles, and in "Tribute to Martin Luther King, Jr." (1976) at the Los Angeles Municipal Art Gallery, reflecting her involvement in black and feminist issues. Her work is now well known throughout the United States. The Pennsylvania Academy of the Fine Arts, Philadelphia, showed a room installation, *Sentimental Sojourn: Strangers and Souvenirs*, in 1987.

Reference The Museum of Contemporary Art, Los Angeles. *Betye Saar*. July 21, 1984–October 7, 1985.

Ball of Fire
1985
Opalescent paints, pastel, colored wire with plastic and metal ornaments, glitter, and sequins on papier-mâché on gauze
17⅜ x 27" (44 x 68.6 cm) composition
1986-52-1

39 FRANK SANSONE

Born 1948, New York?
Studied Pratt Institute, New York
Resides Putney, Vermont

Frank Sansone has participated in group exhibitions at The School of Visual Arts, New York (1971), the Pratt Institute, New York (1972), and the Dayton Art Institute (1978). In 1987 he exhibited at the Catamount Art Center in St. Johnsbury, Vermont.

Three Triangles for Peter V, Grandma Gerbe, and Uncle Lefty
1978
Acrylic on cut paper
30 x 39" (76.2 x 99 cm)
1979-138-1

40 JOEL SHAPIRO

Born 1941, New York
Studied New York University, B.A. 1964; M.F.A. 1969
Resides New York

Joel Shapiro has had numerous solo exhibitions in the United States, and abroad at the Whitechapel Art Gallery, London (1980), The Israel Museum, Jerusalem (1981), and the Stedelijk Museum, Amsterdam, (1985). A traveling retrospective of his work was organized by the Whitney Museum of American Art, New York, in 1982, and another major show was organized by the John and Mable Ringling Museum of Art, Sarasota, Florida, in 1986.

Reference Mark Ormond. *Joel Shapiro: Sculpture and Drawings, 1981–85*. Sarasota, Florida, 1986.

Untitled
1981
Charcoal on wove paper
32⅛ x 39¾" (81.6 x 101.1 cm)
1982-8-1

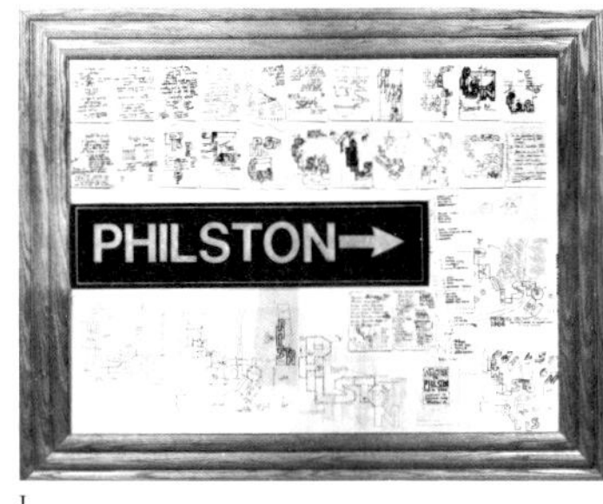

1

3

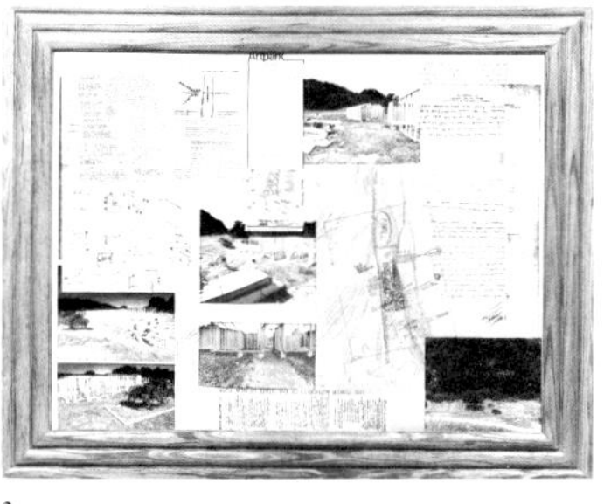

2

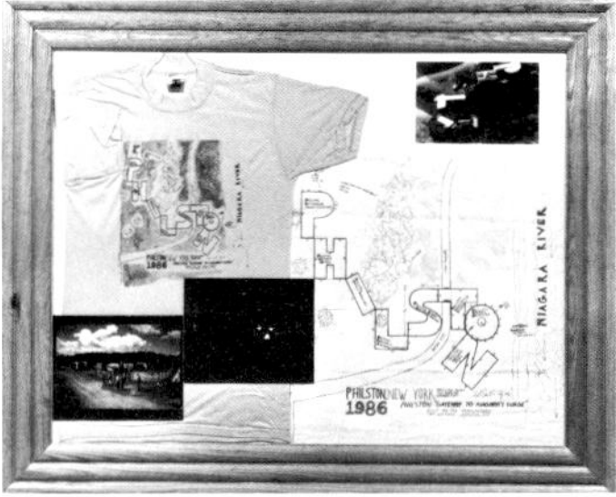

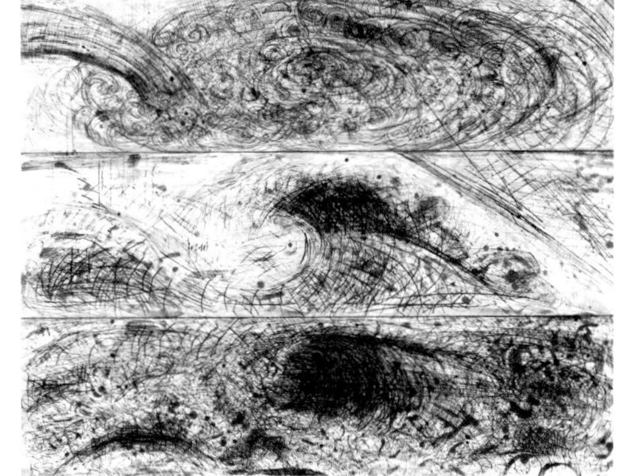

41 PHILLIPS SIMKIN

Born 1944, Philadelphia
Studied Tyler School of Art, Temple University, Philadelphia, B.F.A. 1965
Cornell University, Ithaca, M.F.A. 1967
Teaches York College, City University of New York, and Moore College of Art, Philadelphia
Resides Philadelphia

Phillips Simkin had his first one-man exhibition at Swarthmore College in Pennsylvania in 1970 and has since installed his participatory projects at numerous sites in the United States, including the Institute of Contemporary Art, University of Pennsylvania (1973); the Philadelphia Museum of Art (1974); the Pennsylvania Academy of the Fine Arts (1978); the Institute of Contemporary Art, Boston (1974); Artpark, Lewiston, New York (1975, 1986); PS 1, Long Island City, New York (1976); the Winter Olympics, Lake Placid, New York (1980); and the Capp Street Project, San Francisco (1984). Based on people's spontaneous responses to environments he creates, Simkin's temporary installations or experiential situations draw viewers in as participants interacting with the pieces and each other, challenging traditional conceptions of what is art and mocking the commodity value of the object.

Reference The Temple Gallery, Tyler School of Art, Temple University, Philadelphia. *Phillips Simkin: Daring: A Commissioned Project*. September 25–October 31, 1986.

Philston
1986
Ink, pencil, and white correction fluid on sketchbook paper, architect's tracing paper, blueprint, and graph paper; photocopies; computer printout; silkscreen on cardboard and cotton tee shirt; photographs; typescript; and cibachrome prints mounted on ragboard in oak frames
Three pieces: 38¼ x 47¾" (97.2 x 121.3 cm) each, framed
1988-3-1–3

42 PAT STEIR

Born 1940, Newark, New Jersey
Studied Pratt Institute, Brooklyn, B.F.A. 1962
Boston Museum of Fine Arts School and Boston University, 1958–60
Resides New York and Amsterdam

Pat Steir's work after artists such as Bruegel, Rembrandt, and Van Gogh dates to the mid 1970s. Her first exhibition at a major institution was at the Corcoran Gallery of Art, Washington, D.C., in 1973. Since then she has had numerous solo exhibitions, notably "Form, Illusion, Myth: Prints and Drawings of Pat Steir" (1983), which originated at the Spencer Museum of Art, Lawrence, Kansas. In the past decade Steir has participated in exhibitions in Italy, France, Switzerland, Japan, and The Netherlands.

Reference Elizabeth Broun. *Form, Illusion, Myth: Prints and Drawings of Pat Steir*. Lawrence, Kansas, 1983.

The Wave—From the Sea—After Leonardo, Hokusai, and Courbet
1985
Color etching; edition 50 and 8 artist's proofs
35⅛ x 44½" (89.3 x 113 cm) plate
1987-82-1

43 MICHELLE STUART

Born 1938, Los Angeles
Studied Chouinard Art Institute, Los Angeles, 1954–55
Instituto de Bellas Artes, Mexico City, 1955–56
New School for Social Research, New York, 1958–60
Resides New York

Michelle Stuart first exhibited her paper works in the early 1970s. She has been represented in major group shows, such as "Documenta" (1977) in Kassel, West Germany; "Paper as Medium" (1979), a traveling exhibition organized by the University of Wisconsin, Stevens Point; and "New American Paperwork" (1980), an exhibition that originated at the National Museum of Modern Art, Kyoto. The Hillwood Art Gallery of Long Island University, New York, held a solo exhibition of her work in 1985, and in the same year she participated in "Between the Covers: Handmade Artists' Books" at the Massachusetts College of Art, Boston. In 1986 her huge painting *Paradisi* was exhibited in the Grand Lobby of The Brooklyn Museum.

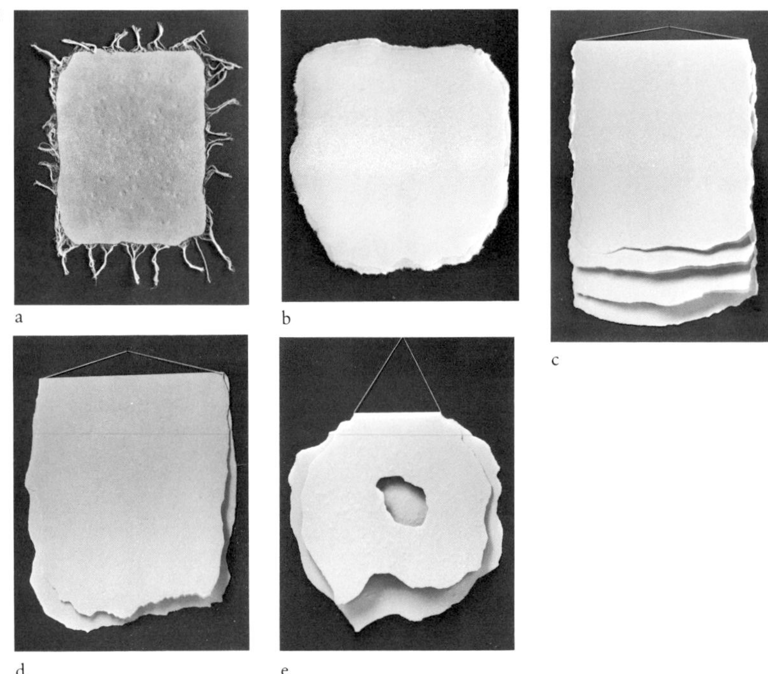

a

b

c

d

e

43 MICHELLE STUART *(continued)*

Reference Hillwood Art Gallery, School of the Arts, Long Island University, New York. *Michelle Stuart: Voyages*. March 20–April 12, 1985.

Tsikomo
1975
Portfolio of five lithographs; edition 24; printed Tamarind Institute, Albuquerque
a) *Tsikupuming*. Color lithograph, tinted cheesecloth, and embossing on Arjomari Arches paper, 13¾ x 11" (35 x 28 cm); b) *Tsikomo*. Lithograph on laminated Copperplate Deluxe and handmade Inomachi Nacre paper with embossing, 15¾ x 14¾" (40 x 37.5 cm); c) *Okuping*. Color lithograph and string on Arches paper, 20½ x 13⅞" (52 x 35.3 cm); d) *Keping*. Color lithograph, string, and embossing on Arjomari Arches paper, 14¾ x 12¾" (37.6 x 32 cm); e) *Kuseping*. Color lithograph, embossing, and string on Arches paper, 13¾ x 13¾" (35 x 35 cm) sheets
1979-139-1a–e

44 ROBERT WILSON

Born 1941, Waco, Texas
Studied Pratt Institute, New York, B.F.A. 1965
Resides New York

Robert Wilson is an internationally known designer, director, and artist, noted in his theater work for scenic illusion and creation of atmosphere. He has received numerous awards for direction and set design and has had many one-man gallery and museum exhibitions of his work, which includes stage design, prints, and drawings. In 1986 his "Parsifal" and "Medea" series of drawings and prints were exhibited at the Lehman College Art Gallery, New York. A retrospective was held in the same year at the Laguna Gloria Art Museum, Austin, Texas.

Reference Galerie Fred Jahn, Munich. *Robert Wilson: Die lithographischen Zyklen, 1984–1986*. 1986.

Parsifal
1985
Nineteen lithographs on various types and sizes of paper; edition 35; printed by Karl Imhof, Munich; published by Fred Jahn, Munich
1986-74-1a–s

45 TERRY WINTERS

Born 1949, Brooklyn
Studied Pratt Institute, New York, B.F.A. 1971
Resides New York

Terry Winters's paintings and graphic works have recently come to national and international attention. One-man exhibitions of his work, which consists of drifting, biomorphic forms, have been held at the Kunstmuseum, Lucerne (1985), The Tate Gallery, London (1986), and the University Art Museum, Santa Barbara, California (1987–88). Among the group shows in which his prints have appeared are the National Print Exhibition (1984, 1986) at The Brooklyn Museum; "Three Printmakers: Jennifer Bartlett, Susan Rothenberg, Terry Winters" (1986) at the Whitney Museum of American Art, New York; and "70s into 80s: Printmaking Now" (1986–87) at the Museum of Fine Arts, Boston. In 1986 an exhibition of Winters's lithographs and drawings was organized by the Yellowstone Art Center, Billings, Montana.

Reference Phyllis Plous. *Terry Winters: Painting and Drawing*. Santa Barbara, California, 1987.

Morula I, II, and III
1983–84
Three color lithographs on handmade Toyoshi paper; editions 38, 37, and 36; printed (by Thomas Cox and Keith Brintzenhofe) and published at Universal Limited Art Editions, West Islip, New York
42 x 32" (106.8 x 81 cm), 42¾ x 32⅜" (108.5 x 82.2 cm), 42¾ x 32⅛" (108.5 x 82.3 cm) sheets
1984-48-1-3

46 ROBERT ZAKANITCH

Born 1935, Elizabeth, New Jersey
Studied Newark School of Fine and Industrial Arts, New Jersey, 1954–57
Resides New York

Robert Zakanitch first exhibited his work in the late 1960s. His reputation as a pattern and decoration painter was well established when he participated in "The Decorative Impulse" (1979), a traveling exhibition organized by the Institute of Contemporary Art, University of Pennsylvania, Philadelphia, where he also had a one-man exhibition in 1981. He exhibited in the Whitney Biennial (1973, 1981) and "American Art since 1970" (1984) at the Whitney Museum of American Art, New York, and his work is currently part of the traveling exhibition "Focus on the Image: Selections from the Rivendell Collection" (1986–90), originating at the Phoenix Art Museum.

Reference Institute of Contemporary Art, University of Pennsylvania, Philadelphia. *Robert S. Zakanitch*. June 12–August 9, 1981.

Double Peacock No. 2
1981
Colored and pressed paper pulp, and watercolor; printed at Tyler Graphics Ltd., Mount Kisco, New York
49 x 36⅛" (124.3 x 91.6 cm)
1981-61-1